THE OBLIGATION
TO DISOBEY

Conscience & the Law

MULFORD Q. SIBLEY

Published by the Council on Religion and International Affairs

FOREWORD

There are times in the histories of nations and of individuals when the most crucial and disturbing issues are most readily perceived in the clash between conscience and the law. We live in such a time now. If our international policies and our domestic policies are not a single, seamless web, they are yet intimately related. And the international issues that have fragmented public opinion are increasingly litigated under different labels in our civil courts.

There are many symposia, conferences, debates, and living-room arguments about the relation of conscience to the law. This essay was initiated by one such gathering. In the fall of 1968 the Council for Philosophical Studies sponsored a conference on "The Responsibilities and Obligations of Citizens and State." As one of the participants, Mulford Q. Sibley was asked to address himself to the topic which is defined by the title of this book. As an interested participant but, even more as director of publications for the Council on Religion and International Affairs, I asked Mr. Sibley to develop some of the most controversial points in his address. CRIA is pleased to publish Mr. Sibley's response to that request.

Mulford Sibley is professor of political science at the University of Minnesota, co-author of *Conscription of Conscience,* a study of American conscientious objectors in World War II, and editor of *The Quiet Battle,* writings on the theory and practice of non-violent resistance.

James Finn
Director of Publications

Council on Religion and
International Affairs

Contents

INTRODUCTION

Ours is a time when all over the world established institutions are being challenged and men are suffering imprisonment for what they allege to be the cause of "conscience." In the Soviet Union, citizens protest repression of liberty and the Soviet invasion of Czechoslovakia. In many parts of Western Europe, university education is being criticized as it never was before. In the United States, the civil rights and peace movements have had their martyrs, many of whom have disobeyed claimed law in the name of supposedly higher principle.

Everywhere the quality of life has been criticized by those who argue that a well-being which is merely economic can never satisfy the human soul. And when we say "quality," we obviously mean something that is not measurable but is, nevertheless, very real. Such criticism involves an appeal to valuations which deal with intangibles, and their expression, in words, is extremely difficult.

Naturally, all this unrest has evoked counter-protest. The "establishment" has reacted in ways which might have been anticipated: by severe repression, by threats, by imprisonment, and by hurling epithets like "irresponsible" and "unpatriotic." Forgetting the long history of dissent, the defenders of the status quo sometimes seem to suggest that deliberate disobedience of law is a new thing. Actually, of course, civil disobedience, dissent, and conscientious defiance of law are very old in the history of human thought and action; but defenders of the existing order in every age tend to believe that their own period is peculiar in its rejection of what the rulers of mankind think is best for the world.

The confrontations of our day raise many questions. On the part of those who challenge the existing structure, such issues as the meaning of conscience, the nature of obligation, the purposes of disobedience, the justifications for dissent, and the temptations of disobedience immediately come to mind. And those who rule are driven to consider the justification for repression, the inherent limitations of law, the ways in which the conscience of the ruler should be shaped, and the issues raised by the inertia of institutions. Law confronts conscience, yet itself represents a kind of conscience. Conscience faces law, but at the same time is often afflicted with uncertainty and ambiguities. The person stands over against state and society, but is himself some kind of an outpost of state and society. The state opposes the person but also, it has been argued, bears the imprint of personality in its very existence.

These are some of the themes of this essay, which seeks, in the first place, to understand conscience and its problems in general; then to examine law with its peculiarities and ambiguities; thirdly, to inquire into the principles which might guide the consciences of citizens and administrators as they seek to determine their obligations to obey or disobey law; and, fourthly, to analyze the nature and complexities of disobedience in general, civil disobedience in particular, and revolution. We conclude with an over-all recapitulation and consider the future of obedience and disobedience.

I. OF CONSCIENCE AND HUMAN PERSONALITY

Obligation signifies that one ought to perform or fail to perform an act because of some moral imperative. Conscience is the voice of that imperative. When we say that we act in a certain way by reason of conscience, we supposedly are not acting out of fear, or because we are intimidated, or for purely self-regarding ends, but because—however we arrive at the judgment—a given course of conduct is morally "right." With respect to civil obedience, the contrast between a non-conscientious and a conscientious act is illustrated—although not fully discussed—in St. Paul's famous admonition to obey the magistrate "not only for wrath, but also for conscience's sake."[1]

Conscience has usually been thought of as the deliverance of a moral judgment in concrete historical circumstances, not simply the enunciation of abstract principles of conduct. To have a conscience about killing or non-killing, we need some set of general propositions. We also need a judgment as to how those principles and priorities are to be applied in particular circumstances such as an actual war, a curious case of "breaking and entering," or an historical instance in which a supposedly berserk person has run amuck and is shooting other persons. There is a steady movement downward—as traditional natural law reasoning has fully recognized—from

[1]Romans 13:6.

the most abstract and general statements (such as "avoid evil and do good") to deductions from those statements, to increasingly specific propositions which take into account such matters as historical circumstances, alternatives available, and weightier versus less weighty moral considerations. An enormous number of factors can be involved before conscience can pronounce judgment at the most concrete level—e.g., "What should I do about obeying the conscription law in the Vietnamese war after it has been waged two years, given my Christian beliefs and the laws of my country?"

But once we have identified conscience in general, we confront the task of giving an account of it—of attempting to understand its ramifications and its relations to us both as individuals and as social beings. Theories about it have varied through the course of the centuries. In the earlier development of thought, apparently, it was regarded as that within a person which gave him pain when he had performed a morally wrong action.[2] Later on, it was conceived as a positive guide to conduct, which not only pronounced against past deeds or warned against future ones but which in addition helped guide the individual in choosing the right. When tradition or mores were no longer implicitly accepted as near-infallible standards, the difficulty of finding criteria for the guidance of conscience became vastly increased.

The etymology of the term itself may give us a clue as to one facet of the controversy about it. Coming from the Latin

[2]The early history of the idea of conscience is discussed in, among other works, C. A. Pierce, *Conscience in the New Testament* (London, 1955).

10

and meaning "joint knowledge," certain earlier conceptions of it appeared to recognize a social content which, in later generations, was sometimes forgotten. One's conscience was, at least in part, one's understanding of the social consensus as to the meaning of right and wrong. Moreover, one's interpretation of the social consensus was itself conditioned by one's social experiences.

On the other hand, there have at times been interpretations which have emphasized the supposedly inner nature of conscience, the implication being that its guidance comes wholly from within the person or at least vertically to the person from God. In this view, judgments of the conscience are those of a kind of discrete individual. The Anglo-Saxon term *inwit* (roughly the equivalent of conscience) would appear to emphasize this interpretation. This view, too, stresses a certain mystery about one's moral deliverances, as if conscience, like God, is beyond understanding. One can only stand in awe of it. It transcends ordinary experience.

Reason + Conscience

Somewhat related to the controversy turning on social versus non-social interpretations has been the conflict between those who regard conscience as somehow apart from reason, and those, on the other hand, who think of it as essentially a reflection of reason. The U.N. Declaration of Human Rights appears to separate "reason" from "conscience."[3] Of course, this may mean simply that conscience goes beyond reason

[3]The exact language of the Universal Declaration of Human Rights (1948) is: "All human beings are born free and equal in dignity and rights. They are endowed with reason and conscience and should act towards one another in a spirit of brotherhood."

and not, necessarily, that it is opposed to reason. But in some versions which appear to separate conscience from reason, the latter seems actually to be opposed to conscience: all of us have heard such statements as, "He acted merely according to human reason," the implication being that reason is a kind of spurious guide for action. Some deeply religious persons seem to be particularly concerned that conscience be regarded as a kind of divine voice having nothing to do with such problems as prediction of consequences and human ratiocination. Although the statement is subject to a variety of interpretations, something like this view appears to be implied in the familiar "I will do right though the heavens fall." Taken literally, this might be viewed as an assertion that one can act in "conscience" even though the results of one's actions are to condemn mankind to utter destruction.

On the other hand, one can associate conscience closely with reason. To be sure, ultimate value judgments—the statement, for example, that in the event of conflict, human life is to be valued above material possessions—may be held to repose on intuitions or on some form of "self-evidence," and hence to go beyond "reason." But in the shaping of a conscience, this view would maintain, reason must necessarily play a vital role; for it must somehow connect the ultimate value judgments with secondary valuations and with the "empirical" world in which the actual alternatives are found. Assessment of alternative results is presumably a function of reason. Medieval moral theologians spoke of "conscience and its casuistry"; in the so-called real world one must often choose between and among alternative courses of action. In the event that given values conflict with one another, one's value system gives one the priorities; but in the application and adaptation of particular means to given ends, one must weigh consequences, and this involves reason and deliberation. One is always torn, of course, between what Max Weber called the "ethic of absolute ends" and the "ethic of responsibility."[4] In the first, we perceive certain things as "right" or "wrong" with little regard for consequences; in the second, we must weigh the consequences of acts as a part of our calculus of decision. The first tends to be the ethic of a certain type of religious view; the second more nearly that of the ethic which a politician follows. In the actual shaping of the conscience, according to the view that "reason" is closely related to conscience, both are involved and necessarily so.

Conscience beyond reason

Here we take the position that all the historically recorded perspectives on conscience have something valid to say to us about the problems of moral experience. Conscience is shaped in a social environment but at the same time must be interpreted by an individual whose ends go beyond those of society. In a very real sense, conscience is "beyond reason" in at least two ways: (1) The ultimate or first-order value judgments are either "intuited" (directly perceived or understood) or, in somewhat other terms, "self-evident." There comes a point, in other words, where "reason" must stop, for its processes themselves proceed from premises which cannot be derived from anything else. Our first-order judgments of value and our ordering of priorities are these premises. (2) The final application of general principles to a particular situation

Value order

[4]See *From Max Weber: Essays in Sociology,* trans. by H. H. Gerth and C. Wright Mills (New York, 1946), pp. 228-35.

is a kind of leap of faith in which our combined rational, empirical, and "beyond reason" propositions are applied to contingent situations. Such an application can never be wholly rational, although it must embrace rational elements if the notion of moral accountability is to have meaning. When we apply general principles to particulars, in light of assessment of consequences and logic, we are and inevitably must be uncertain about how the application should be made. Here, then, reason carries us to the brink; but we must leap across the gorge to action with more than its assistance.

Conscience is thus *both* social and individual; *both* rational (if we accept, in any sense, the "ethic of responsibility") and beyond reason (although we should not make the "beyond reason" into the "irrational" or *against* reason). The person striving to develop a conscience cannot avoid conceptions of right and wrong derived from the past, which are part of his very warp and woof; but if he accepts those conceptions as finally authoritative without question, he is below the level of high conscientiousness. Conscience is the result both of a commitment to faith (at the beginning and in the end) and of the analysis associated with reason (in the middle of its formation). It is obviously affected by our social experience and by the nature of the groups to which we belong; yet simultaneously there is a dimension which transcends the social: it need not be, what some of the Freudians appear to make it, simply a super-ego or deposit of all the *tabus* of the group or groups.

Another way of putting the matter is to see conscience as closely related to consciousness and the problems of moral

14

choice as intimately connected with the nature of human personality. According to *one* view of personality—associated with some organicists, particularly a number of Hegelians—it is simply the "product" of all the values and experiences of the groups out of which it emerges. It is a pale and largely illusory reflection of the "universal" which is the group. Both its weaknesses and its strengths are group-created; and when it thinks, it is the group which is thinking within it. When it is unsure as to how to act—when it is uncertain about what its conscience should be—the experience is simply a reflection of group minds revealed in the so-called individual. When the individual decides how to act (assuming he becomes cognizant of the problem in his subjective consciousness), it is really the predominant group of which he is a member which has decided for him. In a sense, this version would see conscience (at least as usually understood) as an illusion: in reality, there is no "I" but only a seeming conflict of groups acting within "me." In extreme exemplifications of this perspective, the so-called problems of morality are non-existent; we are confronted simply with a question of *describing* accurately how the preponderant group imposes its standards of conduct on the individual (who is under the illusion that, somehow, he is wrestling with his conscience; at most, he is simply trying to understand how he came to the false belief that he was, in some degree at least, an individual).

It is only a *second* view of personality and consciousness which is compatible with the position which we are espousing. This conception would say that while, indeed, the human person cannot develop except in human groups—and thus the purely discrete human individual never existed—groups

15

are only a necessary, but not a sufficient, condition for personality. Groups nourish us spiritually, they provide us with our original points of departure for morality, but potentially each of us is more than all the groups of which he is a part. Groups give us what might be described as the *horizontal* dimension of personality; but its *vertical* aspect goes beyond them and cannot be reduced to them, even though it could not develop without them. The mystery of the human personality lies in the fact that, while it is indeed social, as the organicists contend, it is not *merely* social. Nor is it simply a combination of the genetic and the social.

The person, according to this view, develops in groups, and in the process he becomes aware or conscious of ends, values, goals, and perspectives which he accepts on his own authority, some of which cannot be simply subsumed under the values, ends, and goals of any group or even combination of groups. As this awareness or consciousness grows, the dilemmas, breadth, and depth of conscience grow with it. As the development continues, freedom is enlarged, and with it the puzzles as to how one should act in given circumstances become even greater. Neither this freedom nor these puzzles can be regarded as illusions. With the growth of consciousness comes an enhanced awareness both of separateness and of the ways in which one is tied to other human beings. The greater the breadth and depth of one's awareness, the greater is one's consciousness both of the uniqueness of one's judgments and of the indispensability of society for one's becoming aware.

As the awareness grows, so also does the understanding of the difficulties involved in reaching a truly conscientious decision. The first problem is, of course, to distinguish an act

16

based on conscience from one which is not. The second major issue has to do with developing principles according to which a conscientious act can be performed and which will presumably be more than "subjective" and emotive. A third question involves the problem of applying one's principles to particular and contingent situations, which, as we have seen, is central to the dilemmas of conscience.

In relation to the *first* problem some might argue that the line between a conscientious and a non-conscientious act is so thin as to be virtually non-existent. The vital thing, it might be contended, is the question of substance: to determine the principles which ought to govern all acts and how one can vindicate those principles. The essential issue is to distinguish "right" from "wrong." If there is such an act as a conscientious one, this is less important than that the conscience be a right one. After all, one might have a conscientious Hitler.

But our common language and belief would deny that the distinction between a conscientious and a non-conscientious act is meaningless; and here the common view would appear to be right. What is the quality of "conscientiousness" closely associated with the term "conscience"? We would seem to mean, in the first place, that an act of conscience cannot be separated from the whole pattern of a person's life. Whether an act, in other words, is one of conscience cannot be determined wholly by the claims of the individual or the character of the act itself but only by seeing it in the context of other acts and attitudes revealed by the individual. We may ask, secondly, what this pattern of conscientiousness must be. It should have exemplified, common usage would claim, such

17

qualities as manifest concern for others, assiduousness in performance of duty, a struggle for non-erratic action, candor, openness, and similar qualities—all of them difficult to assess but nevertheless concrete marks of the quality of conscientiousness. The conscientious person has an awareness of obligation to himself, to others, and to society, even though we may differ with him as to precisely what that obligation requires in a particular instance. Conscientiousness signifies seriousness about life. It suggests that we act not merely out of self-concern but also out of concern for others. The conscientious person seeks both an ethic of "absolute ends" and a way in which he can be "responsible" for his acts. He acts not merely out of passion but thoughtfully and deliberately.

When conscientiousness is described in this way, it can be identified, perhaps, with a characteristic which we have often associated with what a human being ought to be, differ though we might with what he decides he ought to do. There is a respect due to "conscientiousness" in itself — the respect which we owe to a human being who is searching for autonomous action, who seeks to build his life on principle, and who is willing to sacrifice for that principle (even if, in our judgment, the principle is wrong-headed).

As for the *second* issue—that of developing principles upon which a conscientious act can be built—the history of moral thought has offered several foundations. Classical natural law doctrine assumes that one can, by examining the "nature" of a thing (both in its primitive sense and in its latent ends), determine what acts are in accordance with nature and hence

18

with the good.[5] The problem is to distinguish between the natural and the unnatural. Kant's principle of universality in the context of the categorical imperative is another purported guide. The Golden Rule, whether in its positive form (do to others what you would like them to do to you) or in its negative expression (do not do to others what you would not have them do to you), represents yet another. The admonition to love one's neighbor (all mankind) as oneself would seem to represent a variant. All statements of this kind have at least one element in common: that we should consider what an act will do not only to the actor but also to others and that others ought to be regarded as having claims as important as those of the actor. Thus, in natural law theory, the natural or good end of each person cannot be entirely divorced from the ends of community.

There is no formulation, however—except perhaps at the very highest level of abstraction (such as "do good, avoid evil")—which will inevitably "coerce" all into accepting it; and even if there were general agreement, this would not necessarily indicate that the formula is objectively "right." The strongest obligation a conscientious man may be said to have is to attempt to discover a principle of action and to work out its implications to the full extent of his ability. Principles —however they may be formulated—do help prevent erratic, unconcerned, or insensitive conduct; and the greater the awareness one has of principles as a guide for action, the greater will be the degree of conscientiousness. To be con-

[5]For a discussion of a modern scholar's interpretation of the ancient origins and meaning of natural law, see John Wild, *Plato's Modern Enemies and the Theory of Natural Law* (Chicago, 1952).

scientious, one must try to formulate such principles as will take account not only of oneself but also of others. This is in part what we mean when we say that "Jones is a principled man." We may not accept Jones's principles and may, indeed, criticize him for them; but the other side of the picture is that we feel impelled to respect him for having principles at all. Principles presumably connect one act with another and provide an integration or wholeness for the personality which would not otherwise be present. What those principles are, of course, is very important. Every conscientious person is obliged to make public the principles which guide him so that others can criticize them; he can take account of the criticisms in any of his re-statements, and wide social agreement may conceivably be reached on standards for conduct. This is at least one dimension of conscience as "joint knowledge" rather than as purely "subjective" guidance.

Third: But as we have suggested earlier, principles must always be applied and it is often very difficult to decide how they relate to a particular case. Generalities and abstractions must become embodied in the world of contingency and flux, and that embodiment entails such judgments as weighing of priorities, prediction of consequences (in terms both of myself and the world of present and future), and what might be called leaps of faith. Let us take a concrete case. A Protestant minister in occupied France during World War II heard that children in the neighborhood were being quizzed by the police as to the presence of Jews. It happened that the minister himself was secluding Jews and assisting them to escape what would be almost certain death in concentration camps. His own children were small and innocent. How should his children respond, he asked himself, to questions about the alleged presence of Jews in his house? If they remained silent, he would be suspect. If they told the truth, he and his children would be accessories to murder (at least as he viewed the matter). If his children lied in such a plausible way that the police would be thrown off the track, the Jews might be saved but another commandment would be seriously violated. Finally, the minister decided he must take the last course of action: he trained his children to lie in a persuasive way, so that Jews could be smuggled out of the country. Then on Sunday—one supposes—he would preach sermons praising truth-telling and respect for life. In making this decision, he had to weigh the sin of killing against that of lying—for, from the human perspective, it seemed to be a choice between the two. He had also to consider seriously the impact on his children of deliberately training them to lie: Being very sensitive, how would this affect their future? What obligation did he owe to the questioners, who, after all, were human beings, albeit engaged on a mission which was pernicious? In the end, his decision involved a kind of over-all intuitive judgment which attempted to take into account the hierarchy of his principles, the concrete situation, and possible effects on others and himself. However, this calculus could not be exact—it involved insights beyond precise analysis but which yet took analysis into consideration.

Two men can conscientiously begin with the same formulation of principles (natural law, Kantian, Golden Rule, or combinations and expansions of these) and, logically, go part of the way together in the application of those principles. They ought, of course, to follow reason as far as it will clearly take them, for irrationality is not a part of "conscience." But in the end, they may differ about how the common principles should be applied to the whole complex of a contingent situation. Thus another minister might, beginning with the Ten Commandments and the New Testament, have reached a conclusion different from that of the Protestant minister in France.

Dietrich Bonhoeffer was an articulate and conscientious Christian during World War II, who eventually concluded that it might be one's duty to kill Nazi leaders.[6] Other apparently equally conscientious Christians could, and did, reach an opposite conclusion: as pacifists, they could not sanction deliberate killing, whatever the supposed end. Both Bonhoeffer and those who took an opposing position were *conscientious* as that term is used here and, indeed, as it is employed generally; yet the substance of one conscience appeared to approve killing under particular circumstances while the other disapproved. Both Bonhoeffer and those who disagreed with him could be distinguished from the non-conscientious who obeyed the regime without thought, who rationalized acts which they did not really approve, who integrated themselves around the goals of plunder, or who allowed their conduct to be determined by the passions of the moment.

When one comes to judge the morality of acts, we are contending, a certain great respect is due to those who act conscientiously, even if we differ sharply with the deliverances of

[6]Eberhard Bethge writes of the July, 1944 abortive attempt on Hitler's life, that "The failure of the plot was a dreadful blow for Bonhoeffer . . ." Editor's Foreword to Dietrich Bonhoeffer, *Letters and Papers from Prison* (New York, 1953), p. 12. Earlier, Bethge tells us, Bonhoeffer had abandoned his near-pacifism.

those consciences and with the principles which presumably govern them. A person who "wrestles with his conscience," as we often say, is a human being at the higher levels of humanity, even though we may have to censure the acts which that conscience leads him to commit. He is to be sharply contrasted with all those who act merely out of habit, or simply because the law or an official requires a given act (without pronouncing on the justice or injustice of the act itself), or merely for personal gain. Acting conscientiously, both in its subjective and its objective sense, and alike on its rational and its non-rational levels, is to be respected by all those who value civil society, the principles of moral autonomy, and the slow growth of man from the status of being an unreflective, passive being to the position of one who seeks to be self-governing in every sense of that term.

But in placing this high valuation on conscience as such, we are sometimes told that we are in effect undermining another dimension of supposed self-government and civilization—that of law and its related institutions. How, it might be asked, can conscience, as here conceived and defined, be reconciled with the law, which not infrequently may command acts that fly in the face of an individual's deeply held sense of right? Before we can answer this question, we must turn to law itself and note the diverse ways in which it has been viewed during the history of human thought.

II. OF LAW'S PECULIAR STATE

Positive law, of course, may take many forms. It may be public or private; civil or criminal; contractual or customary; judicially defined or legislatively promulgated. At the outset, we should recognize its multitude of reflections and not attempt to reduce its many-faceted nature to one type only: we should not, for example, identify "law" merely with criminal law, as some tend to do. Whatever it is—and its precise definition has always troubled students of jurisprudence—it would appear to be ubiquitous. In one way or another, every human being is touched by it and, if he is to develop a conscience, must formulate some kind of attitude to it.

Our attitudes to law historically have been mixed. Sometimes we utter the expression "the rule of law" as if it were the highest level of understanding reality. We often forget that, in the long history of speculation, men have been torn between a position which would see law as a kind of gutter method of social control and, on the other hand, a view which would exalt it as the epitome of human achievement. Without an understanding of our divided mind on this subject, the dilemmas of obedience and disobedience of law are seen in too narrow a perspective. For our obligation to obey law will necessarily be conditioned by the role which we conceive it to play in human life.

Law has often been seen as a kind of cumbrous and sometimes cruelly unjust device. It was not a modern S.D.S. member or a hippie who wrote:

> The law does not perfectly comprehend what is noblest and most just for all and therefore cannot enforce what is best. The differences of men and actions, and the endless irregular movements of human things, do not admit of any universal and simple rules. And no art whatsoever can lay down a rule which will last for all time.
>
> ... The law is always striving to make one—like an obstinate and ignorant tyrant, who will not allow anything to be done contrary to his appointment, or any questions to be asked—not even in sudden changes of circumstances, when something happens to be better than what he commanded for someone ...
>
> A perfectly simple principle can never be applied to a state of things which is the reverse of simple.[7]

When Plato uttered these words, he was speaking for what would become a major tradition in political thought as well as for an important part of our common popular consciousness. Because law must be expressed in terms of categorizations and, to be universal, must make distinctions far fewer than the number of souls to be ruled; because general positive rules always lag behind changes in actual social conditions; because promises to act in a certain way at a future date (as in contracts) may run counter to one's highest moral obligations at the time the promises are supposed to be fulfilled—for these and other reasons there has always been a discrepancy between what positive law demands and what exact righteous-

[7]*Statesman,* Jowett translation, 294, a,b.

ness might entail. And sometimes the discrepancy becomes enormous indeed.

Every human being, in his uniqueness, finds himself entrapped by legal categories and by the complicated and often seemingly absurd procedures associated with positive law. If a Solon or a Bentham appear to sweep away the old cobwebs, new ones rapidly take their place. Try as it will to increase the number of its classifications and the subtleties of its distinctions, attempt as it does to provide equitable remedies, law can never do justice to that dimension of personality which transcends the social and which sees its obligation in somewhat different terms from those of other equally unique personalities. Like a literary rebel who rejects conventional prose and verse forms, every individual at times is rightly tempted to revolt against the kind of order which even the best legal system enshrines. Even in matters which personalities have in common—the public good or the common welfare —the consciousness and conscience of every soul may be unique in awareness of what the public good demands and what the good entails for a given person.

Nor is this dubiety about law confined to any one school of thought. We have cited Plato. We might also have referred to the anarchist William Godwin, who in his great treatise on *Political Justice* deals at length with the problem of law and, curiously enough, in a way which is up to a point very similar to Plato's.[8] Godwin sees the "right" for every man as varying from circumstance to circumstance, since general principles

[8]In *Political Justice* (1793), Godwin sees law as a kind of pretentious fraud which is always getting in the way of an individual's being righteous.

26

must be applied to widely different concrete situations. To promise to obey a law in the future, therefore—whether it be enacted by the legislature or by agreement between individuals in the form of a contract—is immoral; for promises of this kind say in effect that I will act in a certain way even though my insight into the morally right at the time may run directly contrary to what the promise demands. No legal device can take precedence over my insight into the principles of right and wrong and the way that they should be applied in concrete circumstances.

Moreover, although the law may aspire to do exact justice, there is much validity in the Marxist argument that, while it purports to be impartial as between and among individuals and classes, it is in effect an instrument to promote the economic and status interests of the ruling class. In modern American society, of course, the whole system of property relations is defined by law; but it is defined in such a way that speculation in scarce land and natural resources is encouraged, serious tax loopholes for the rich are created, and, despite lip-service to the contrary, centralization of economic power in the hands of the few is not effectively inhibited. Land speculation means that a handful of men can hold land until its community-created value goes up, whereupon the law allows them to reap this socially added price. Although a graduated income tax law seems to be fair, it is loaded with so many qualifications and special privileges (most of which benefit the rich who can afford clever attorneys to discover the tax loopholes) that thousands of the elite pay relatively low taxes. While laws ostensibly attempt to check concentration of economic power, their administration has been such and the existing power of corporate interests so great that the laws are relatively ineffective. The legal system enshrines a property scheme which permits a distribution of income not too different in 1955 from what it was in 1910.[9] All these characteristics of modern America are buttressed and defended by its laws. Can it be wondered, then, that radicals exalting the principle of equality see law as an instrument for maintaining injustice while at the same time pretending to sustain equity?

Some of the greatest literary utopias, it is instructive to note, have abolished law and the legal profession. Thus H. G. Wells' *Men Like Gods* is characterized by a form of anarchy.[10] The English Peasants' Revolt in the latter part of the fourteenth century was characterized by its attacks on lawyers, as was the Peasants' War in Germany during the early portion of the sixteenth.[11] Law and the lawyers were seen as essentially defenders of exploiting landlords and their hangers-on. Much later on, social reformers like Jeremy Bentham were

[9]For a detailed analysis of the distribution of economic power in the United States, see Ferdinand Lundberg, *The Rich and the Super-Rich* (New York, 1968).

[10]Wells sees an ideal society in which men are freed from trammels of the law, which is viewed as an unnecessary yoke. The work of the world somehow gets done without formal rules and coordination. Individuals simply see what needs to be done and do it; and their efforts mesh sufficiently well.

[11]During John Ball's rebellion in the fourteenth century, the law was seen by the rebels as an important buttress of distorted economic power, and lawyers were regarded as the "fixers" and manipulators who sustained an unjust economic order. On the rebellion of the German peasants, see Friedrich Engels, *The Peasant War in Germany* (New York, 1926).

given to such memorable utterances as: "The most difficult task on earth would be to change an English lawyer into an honest man."[12]

Much of this protest, to be sure, was rooted in objections to the usually esoteric language which expresses and colors the law. In every age, law and lawyers, like the priests, are partly hidden by a veil of mystery—and this in itself tends to promote antagonism. The conservative nature of the legal profession, moreover, comports poorly with the demands of desperate men seeking justice. To the demands of the latter, the legal profession can suggest—and quite rightly—that unless due process is observed, injustice may become even greater.

Nevertheless, the image of the law held by millions of human beings throughout history has been of an institution shrouded by hocus-pocus, defended by mumbo-jumbo, and sustaining the unjust; and both lawyers and judges have been seen very much as they are portrayed by Charles Dickens in his great novel *Bleak House*.[13]

Yet there is another and quite different attitude to the law which is as significant as the first position. It maintains that although the law must necessarily fall far short of righteousness, it can at least rise above sheer tyranny. While it may admittedly enshrine many injustices, it tends to prevent the

[12]Bentham's great treatise *Fragment on Government* (1776) was essentially an attack on the jurist William Blackstone and on conceptions of law associated with men like Blackstone.

[13]In *Bleak House*, the equity case Jarndyce v. Jarndyce drags on for a generation, enriching lawyers and depleting the estate which was the subject of the litigation.

most egregious injustice of all: arbitrarily exercised power, whether of public rulers or of private persons. If it were within the domain of the possible for righteousness to be administered in each unique situation by men who were perfectly wise and not subject to gusts of passion and self-interest, argues Plato, then the very existence of law would seem to be the outrage it has appeared to be. But the fact is that no such men can be found; and in their absence, law must be regarded as a second-best instrument for governance.

The ideal ruler, Plato goes on, the ruler with wisdom enough to govern without law, is like the pilot directing the movements of a ship:

> As the pilot, by watching continually over the interests of the ship and of the crew—not by laying down rules, but by making his art a law—preserves the lives of his fellow-sailors, even so, and in the self-same way, may there not be a true form of polity created by those who are able to govern in a similar spirit, and who show a strength of art which is superior to law?[14]

But Plato answers his own question negatively. He has searched throughout his life for men who could guide the body politic without succumbing to the temptations of tyranny and arbitrary rule, and he has never found such men. And his attitude has been echoed by a long tradition since ancient times: by Aristotle, Cicero, Bracton, John of Salisbury, Locke, the American founding fathers, and many others.

Plato's rather melancholy acceptance of law as a grim necessity serves as a reminder to us: while all of us, as thinking men, become impatient with the law and see it as frequently

[14]*Statesman,* Jowett translation, 297.

a distortion of justice, most of us eventually come to accept it, in at least a qualified way, as the best arrangement possible under the circumstances. We live with it, as we live with many of the inconveniences of nature, in order to reap its relative benefits.

Writing from the viewpoint of a Christian perspective, St. Augustine reminds us strongly of Plato. Looking at the problem of man in political society as partly one of defining legitimate authority in collective matters, he suggests that in the pure sense there can be no valid authority in history and that it is often difficult to distinguish between a robber band and a so-called state. All claimed authority, whether among pirates or in states, tends to aggrandize itself, to blaspheme God, to identify itself with divinity, to become aggressive, and to be absorbed in the ends of those who wield it rather than in the common ends for which it ostensibly exists. "Without true righteousness," asks the saint, "what is a state but a band of robbers?"[15] Since true righteousness is never even approximated, the answer would seem obvious and our obligation to obey the laws of the state would be similar to our duty, if any, to observe the laws of a robber band which has made us captive. Is one really obliged to obey the rules of a pirate chief? And is not the ruler of a "Great Power" very much like a pirate chief, in that he preys on lesser powers, seeks a disproportionate share of the economic resources of the earth, and is forever disturbing the tranquility of others?

Yet for the Bishop of Hippo, as for Plato, there is another

[15]His discussion of the whole question is dispersed among several chapters of *The City of God*. See Book II, Chap. 21; Book IV, Chap. 4; and Book XIX, Chaps. 21, 23, and 24.

side to the coin. While every historical state resembles a robber band, it is also true that every group of robbers has many of the same objectives as the state. The state is in some respects an association of pirates writ large; and a band of pirates is the state writ small. As the state must have laws to distribute scarce (or economic) resources, so must the robber band have rules to allocate spoils; as the state attempts to establish a system for the distribution of honors, so must the association of robbers; as the state needs an order within which its citizens can act, so too does the aggregation of pirates. While a commonwealth in the true sense would be a multitude of people bound together by the pursuit of common ends and a commitment to righteousness, historically we probably have to settle for the relative legitimacy of any aggregation of people bound together by the pursuit of common ends—and the ends might or might not have any congruence with justice. In the second-level definition of Augustine's commonwealth, the "justice" is dropped, and order—for the ends of the objects of the group's love—becomes the central value.

Thus every state and every system of positive law will hang between the pole of righteousness, on the one hand, and the lack of any order whatsoever, on the other. States will constantly be violating the standards of righteousness and running roughshod over unique personalities, yet at the same time will be contributing something of value if they develop even a very rough ordering of things. From this point of view, Augustine would seem to be saying, a powerful association of robbers may possess a kind of "legitimacy" if it substitutes order for incipient chaos; for though the goal of ordering may be the plundering of those outside the association, the implementing

32

of the goal will inevitably necessitate certain boons—a system of law, for example, and a scheme of allocation for economic goods.[16]

Augustine's point is amply illustrated if we examine the structure of organized crime in the United States. The Cosa Nostra, for example, resembles a state: there are definite policy-making bodies, policy-executing departments, and clearly defined responsibilities for members. Physical force is used as a sanction both within the organization and against those who are not members. There is a scheme for allocating goods and a system of supposed justice, within which each member has his allotted role. What, we may well ask, is the Cosa Nostra if not a state, with all the prerogatives of a state?[17] To be sure, it is at war, we say, with "organized society." But is not every major state also at war with its leading rivals? From the viewpoint of an incipient world community, every so-called state is a special-interest group seeking through conflict to get as much from others as possible—through currency manipulations, control of resources, and, on occasion, both hot and cold war.

It would appear, then, that the Platonic and Augustinian views are strikingly similar to each other. They point in the

[16]In Charles E. Merriam's *Political Power* (New York, 1934), Chap. III, "Law Among the Outlaws," there is an extensive treatment of the parallels between the law of the state and the law of a gangster organization.

[17]See the discussion of La Cosa Nostra in *The Challenge of Crime in a Free Society:* A Report By the President's Commission on Law Enforcement and Administraton of Justice (Washington, D.C., 1967), pp. 192-96. On p. 194, there is a chart of organization, which reveals a striking parallel to the organization of the "state"—including groups called "soldiers."

same direction: every historic ordering (whether Cosa Nostra or states) will violate human personality and righteousness and also support an arrangement of social relations which will be morally justifiable, given historic possibilities. Every ordering may reflect justice in a kind of distorted way and many will aspire to a more than distorted version; yet whatever the aspiration, the power of money, status, bureaucratic structures, and special interests will always tend to frustrate the thrust to equity and righteousness. Law, as a mirror of both customary and legislative value judgments and social practices, will portray these ambivalences and contradictions. As an attempt to state authoritative norms for what is expected of men, it will often reach upward toward justice, only to be pulled downward by the weight of economic and social power differentiations.

The Platonic and Augustinian views would seem to be—despite possible exaggerations at points—fairly accurate representations of our social and political experience. We shall, therefore, assume a considerable measure of validity in their portrayals as we explore the questions of obligation and disobedience against the background of man's complicated experience of conscience. In carrying forward the exploration, we should keep in mind the many-sided nature of conscience as well as the curiously uncertain and ambivalent position of law. Judgments of right and wrong in particular circumstances are notoriously difficult to make; yet there is an important distinction to be made between actions based on such explicit judgments and actions performed out of mere habit, or dictated by momentary passions, or motivated by self-interest, or carried out without serious attempts to deliberate. Actions

34

under the aegis of some effort to develop a conscience are to be respected as a tribute to man's quest for rationality as well as to his emerging moral sense—even though we may disapprove the substance of the actions. Similarly, although law is in the unenviable position of never being able to reflect pure justice and is, indeed, often highly colored by the reverse, yet because it aspires to justice and generally speaking is to be preferred to a life without law, it is entitled to a certain reverence.

But what ought we to do as we seek to develop an awareness of our obligations to obey or disobey? What are the principles which might guide both the citizen and the administrator in the shaping of their consciences?

III. INDIVIDUAL CONSCIENCE AND THE LAW

We contend that the individual alone must ultimately be responsible for deciding whether or not to obey the law. He alone will have to go through the difficult process of deciding where his obligation begins and ends; and only he, in the last analysis, can interpret whatever general principles he has adopted for the guidance of his conscience. To be sure, the principles and applications of others can be of enormous help, and he is morally obliged to take them into consideration as he wrestles with the problems of obligation. He ought never to act in such a way that he does not recognize his kinship to others and the fact that, in acting, he is in one sense performing as an agent of a humanity he would like to see. But in the end, assuming he wishes to be both responsible and free, he alone must make the decision.

This general position has often been challenged in recent years. Thus Dr. Will Herberg once asserted:

Every man has his conscience; and if the individual conscience is absolutized (that is, divinized), and made the final judge of laws to be obeyed or disobeyed, nothing but anarchy and the dissolution of the very fabric of government would result.[18]

And the late President Kennedy was once quoted to the effect

18Will Herberg, "A Religious 'Right' to Violate the Law?" *National Review* (July 14, 1964), p. 580.

that Americans were not "free" to choose the laws they should obey.[19]

There is, to be sure, an ambiguity about such statements. It is not always clear how the word "conscience" is being used, for example; and "individual conscience" might conceivably mean "erratic or haphazard choice." What, moreover, do we mean when we say that individuals are not "free" to choose the laws which are to be obeyed? Do we mean, for example, that they do not have the capacity? Or do we mean that they have no moral "right" to decide when and when not to disobey?

If Herberg is using the word "conscience" in somewhat the same way we have been employing it, his statement would seem difficult to support. For, we might ask, if the individual conscience is not to be the "final judge" of the laws to be obeyed or disobeyed, who or what is? We are not told. If the judgment is to be made by a divine book of some kind, then we must immediately ask who is to interpret the book. Surely, in the end, the individual conscience must do so. But perhaps the decision as to when to obey or disobey is to be rendered by a church. If so, however, who gives authority to the church? In the last analysis, the individual himself must have assented to the church becoming the trustee for his conscience; and if he has not in fact done so, he has no conscience, at least as we are using the term. If a judicial court is to perform the mission, what is the individual to do if he regards the interpretation of the court as utterly mistaken? Obey the

[19]See the *New York Times* (October 1, 1962), p. 22. Statements of this kind seem to have taken on the qualities of dogmas which none might question.

court rather than his own judgment of right and wrong? If so, why? To answer this question, he would in turn have to develop a conscientious view about allowing the court to act for him. There would seem ultimately to be no alternative to the individual conscience.

To be sure, Herberg legitimately warns us against "absolutizing" or "divinizing" whatever the conscience may say. It is, indeed, dangerous to assert that because one must act according to one's conscience, the pronouncements of the conscience are the "voice of God." Those pronouncements, we may say, are only the dictates of what we deem to be right at a given time and under particular circumstances after a long process of deliberation and intuition. They may be "wrong" in the sense that our apprehension of what righteousness demands may not accord with "reality." We may not see the "form" of righteousness clearly or may apply it in a way which is objectively wrong. We should always be aware of this. "By the bowels of Christ," Cromwell told Parliament on one occasion, "I beg you to remember that you may be wrong." Certainly such an admonition is always needed for every conscience, however carefully it may have been formed. If we say that we must allow our consciences to tell us when to obey and disobey, we do so with awareness that they may prove to be voices of the devil rather than of God. Nevertheless, no other persons or groups at the time can authoritatively tell us that this is so, although they may and should express their views. Finally, the individual conscience must judge, for to refuse to do so would be to reject both freedom and responsibility. If someone suggests that we should indeed reject freedom and responsibility forever, there is nothing, of course, that we can say in reply, except to observe that one is in effect willing one's own slavery.

We may not be satisfied with the statement that the individual conscience must be the ultimate judge—we shall no doubt continue to repeat such clichés as "if the individual can decide which laws he will obey, the foundations of society will be destroyed"—but there would seem to be no alternative, short of denying individual moral responsibility. Some may suggest, to be sure, that if my conscience is "wrong" (as we have admitted it may be), there is no obligation to follow it. But if I do not see that it is "wrong," I would be renouncing my responsibility and freedom *not* to follow it; for in effect I would be saying that a majority or a special group can tell me to do what I think is not right for me to do. St. Thomas Aquinas rightly said long ago that one must follow one's conscience, even if it is objectively wrong.[20]

What are we to say of Herberg's contention that if individual conscience is followed, "nothing but anarchy . . . would result"? If by "anarchy" he means that uniformities of action or expectation that now appear to be necessary might be put in jeopardy, we should have to admit that he is right. But this is an inevitable risk if we commit ourselves to man's freedom and responsibility. The alternative would be a form of slavery, which would be an even greater hazard.

The "nothing but" in Herberg's proposition, however, is unsupportable; for following conscience may lead either to conformity or to non-conformity. Often we tend to associate the word only with the latter, perhaps because so many conform not by reason of conscience but because of uncriticized

[20]*Summa Theologica,* First Part of II, Q. IX, Art. 5; *Quodlibet,* 27.

39

and unexamined habit or as a result of fear. But there is no reason why some uniformity in conduct could not also result from pursuit of conscience; and, indeed, this would presumably be the ideal. Even from the military point of view, no doubt, it would be better if most of the men in Vietnam were fighting because their consciences dictated this action rather than because—as is true in actual fact—they were coerced by opinion or fears, or conformed simply because most others were doing the same. Military morale would be much higher if every soldier had joined because of conscientious conviction. And conscientious obedience to law is better because, in general, it is likely to be less superficial and more in accordance with the spirit of the law than is non-conscientious obedience—which is the fruit of fear or the mechanical following of habit or sheer sheep-like conformity to what one's peers are doing.

Suppose, though, that one man's provisional conscience tells him to violate the law by assassinating a prominent political leader and that mine tells me that such an act is morally wrong. Should each of us act in accordance with his own particular conscience? To revert to a previous example, should both those who supported Bonhoeffer's position on political assassination and those whose consciences led them to pacifism have acted in their sharply contrasting ways? This is apparently the kind of situation envisioned by Will Herberg when he warns us against "absolutizing" the individual conscience.

In attempting to answer the question, we should recall our observation[21] that conscience of any kind implies awareness

21See pp. 17-18.

of social responsibility and a willingness to consider the views of others in shaping one's own dictate of obligation. In the case we are considering, the conscientious assassin would, no doubt, consult me (or someone with my views, or, in Germany, those conscientiously opposed to assassination) before proceeding to execute his tentative judgment. I and others would "reason" with him, as we say, and would also exchange with him non-rational (but not irrational) insights into the nature of the moral order. We should not discount this process of joint consultation as a way of reaching agreement and avoiding a kind of solipsism.

We might agree on our general first-order insights into the nature of the moral principles involved but differ as to how they should be applied; for, as we have seen earlier,[22] there may be widespread agreement on basic moral propositions but, beyond a certain point, wide differences about how they should be applied to particular contingencies. In the present case, it might be possible through a combination of exchanges of general moral experience and reasoning to reach consensus that assassination is an immoral or at least an inappropriate means; whereupon the potential assassin's tentative conscience would have changed. For the most part, as a matter of fact, reason and intuition hold men together at least as much as they divide them, so that the experience of final agreement imagined here could be said to be a very common one.

Suppose, however, that his provisional conscience was not changed as the result of our dialogue or that—even worse—we could not agree on the general premises which should govern moral reasoning (this latter is unlikely, particularly

[22]See pp. 20-22.

at the very abstract level, but is still a possibility). What, then, would be our respective obligations? If we assume, as we are assuming, that both of our consciences were the result of serious deliberation and testing, then each of us would have to go his own way—he to the gun-store and I, perhaps, to the police. There is no doubt that such an eventuality is possible (although not as probable, perhaps, as some like Herberg might imagine), even though I might decide, if I were a German pacifist living in Nazi Germany, that I had no obligation to go to the police. But if we accept, as we do, St. Thomas' principle of following one's conscience even though it be objectively wrong, then there is nothing else to do.

Thus exchange of experiences and reason might or might not lead to a confluence of consciences. But if those whose tentative judgments differed initially had sought to work out the implications of conscientiousness and conscience with respect to obedience or disobedience, what kinds of principles would they have discerned? Accepting the general notions of conscientiousness and conscience, and the framework of judgments about law examined earlier, how might two potentially differing consciences have sought to spell out in some detail their obligations to obey or disobey law?

Before answering this question, it is well to emphasize that, while the formulation of such principles may be expected to expand our consciousness and provide greater joint knowledge, we should not expect too much. In the end, as Rudolph H. Weingartner has argued, we can never discover a "simple way" of dealing with the ethics of obedience and disobedience.[23] There will always be many "ifs" and "buts," and this would seem to be an inevitable accompaniment of the quest for conscientious action and, if possible, objectively "right" action. Nevertheless, principles are indispensable if we are to avoid the even greater pitfalls associated with non-conscientious conduct.

A preliminary point: while the principles themselves will be useful in the shaping of a conscience on any issue, our center of attention will be the problem of a conscience about obedience or disobedience to specific positive laws. It will be assumed, for the most part, that the legal system as a whole is not in question but rather that the problem is one of obedience to particular laws. In the process, of course, the nature of any legal system will have to be adverted to and the question of the legitimacy of recognizing the legal system while rejecting given enactments must inevitably be explored.

What, then, is one morally obliged to do before settling on a conscientious conviction about conformity or non-conformity to a particular law? We offer these considerations: (1) Legal obligation roots in a broad conception of moral obligation, which in turn must be related to the social nature of man. (2) Social life is pluralistic, and this must be taken into account when formulating a conscience on a particular question. (3) There is an obligation to humanity. (4) State law does not necessarily have any greater claim on me than other forms of law, including the legislation I enact for myself. (5) One should test one's tentative judgments according to several criteria.

[23]Rudolph H. Weingartner, "Justifying Civil Disobedience," *Columbia University Forum* (Spring, 1966), p. 42.

1. *Personality, the Group, and Obligation.* Any discussion of obligation must consider the nature of human personality and its relation to the groups so vital in its development. One cannot be oneself or be born as a person without groups and the orderings of group life. An understanding of this fact should lead me to recognize that I could not be myself without the groups into which I was born. If I affirm the high value of human life—and this affirmation would seem to be a prerequisite for any discussion of obligation—then a consciousness of my obligation to the sources of life would appear to be implied. Just as we have an indebtedness to our biological parents and ancestors for the gift of life which we share, so we are indebted to multifarious social groupings for being able to transcend merely biological or vegetative existence to become persons. We become conscious that each of us is a child of the group as each is also the offspring of physical parents. Recognition of social obligation is awareness of a basic element in justice or righteousness: giving to each his due.

One principle which would seem to be implied in this recognition of social obligation is the sacred character of human life—others' as well as my own. We are to respect human life as an end in itself and all our actions must be related to this central value. The admonition to love one's neighbor as oneself, although it may be expressed in varying ways, is a near-universal heritage of man's moral consciousness—and one which is constantly re-affirmed by our intuitions. When I am told to love my neighbor as myself, it does not mean that I love him *because* I love myself but rather that concern for oneself and one's neighbor are mutually supportive: active good will for my neighbor is a necessary condition for a self-love which is not destructive; and good will toward myself entails the self-respect without which good will for my neighbor is watery, erratic, and easily transformed into destructive hatred. Without love, there is no community; and without community the very notion and possibility of human life tends to be destroyed. "The starving dog at his master's gate," William Blake once said, "bespeaks the ruin of the State." My obligation to the groups which helped me on the road to personhood is related to a like obligation to respect and love their members.

But if I am to respect the group and love its members, I am equally obliged, in general, to respect the rules which seem to be a necessary condition for group life; and it is these rules to which we often give the name "law." We must value law and see it, to some extent at least, as a factor without which human social existence and therefore human life could not be. This obligation exists even though we recognize all the ambivalences and problems of law which we have suggested earlier. The general obligation applies not only to the law of the state but also to the laws generated by other groups and associations of which I am a member.[24] From this point of view, law is the second-best effort to order the life of any association or group, so that it can carry on its legitimate functions and the member can be provided a framework of expectations within which to act as a member of the group. As I acknowledge my debt to the group, so must I recognize

[24]Obviously, this is to adopt a "pluralist" notion of law, for which one need make no apologies. To be sure, the state law may insist that it takes precedence, in the event of a conflict, over the laws of other associations; but that is merely its word, and, like other provisions of the law, must be judged by the individual.

a certain sense of fealty to the rules which express its life.

This does not mean, however, that law is the most valuable element in life. Although I may give it high rank and see it as of enormous import in the tangled skein of historical existence, I shall also value friendship and spontaneous action and contemplation and countless other dimensions of experience whose claims on me may, at times, conflict with my obligations to positive law. The contents of law, too, may not infrequently belie the purposes which law ostensibly should serve: to assist in providing a framework in which social solidarity, love, and human personality can most fully develop. My only absolute obligation is to righteousness, as I see it at my highest possible level of consciousness; and righteousness is somehow related to giving all constituents of human life— individual and social—their full due, against the background of the admonition to love. Law is one, but only one, of those constituents.

2. *Plurality of Groups and the Obligation to Obey Law.* Each of us finds his circumstances complicated, of course, because he is a member of many groups and associations, of which the state is merely one. I belong to a religious association which nourishes my spiritual life; to economic groups which reflect my interests as a producer or consumer; to tribe-like and clan-like aggregations; and to many others. Each expresses its life, in part, through law. While the sanctions of the several laws may differ—the church excommunicates or fines, the state imprisons, the athletic association expels or censures, and so on—essentially the roles and functions of the laws are similar; and in every case they share the limitations we have suggested.

46

If, as a conscientious person, I am compelled (because of a conflict between and among the diverse laws of groups) to choose the laws which shall claim my allegiance, I may be required to reject the binding quality of some while affirming others. I may at times place the law of the state above that of my church; and at other times, as in the case of the conscientious St. Thomas More, may do the reverse. As a morally accountable human being, conscientiousness compels me to do this; I cannot evade the responsibility nor is there any formula whereby an association, court, or authority figure can resolve the problem for me.

3. *Obligation to Humanity*. Although the idea of humanity as a group or association is a vague one and we may argue that the human race has no positive laws as such, still I cannot ignore the fact that I am a member of the human race, and this group too may be said to have incipient laws. At any rate, I can and must attribute to it a striving for expression through law, and, in the event of conflict, weigh its claims against those of other groups and associations. If I think of the Geneva convention on the use of gas in warfare as positive law, for example, I am bound to consider its imperatives as over against the commands of American laws requiring me to enter an army which uses gas in Vietnam.

International law, in general, can perhaps be regarded as a kind of latent world positive law, even though in form it may not be because it does not directly apply to individuals.[25]

---

[25]Here we are making a distinction between so-called public international law, which regulates the relations of nation-states with one another, and a potential world law, which would be applied to *individuals* throughout the globe.

Although the so-called Great Powers, in particular, flout many parts of international law, this does not excuse me from considering whether it is binding in principle on me. In the last analysis, we are contending throughout, the individual conscience must judge both what is law and what is bad law.

4. *State Law, Non-State Law, and Individual Purposes.* I am an officer—that is, occupy a social role—in many groups and associations, the claims of which must sometimes be weighed against one another in light of a value and priorities system which states my understanding of the objective moral order. We have suggested that the central principle of this order would seem to be respect for all human life, with all other values subordinate to it.

But since I am not merely an officer of associations and groups but also a being transcending the social dimension, I must weigh the claims of groups and associations not only against one another but also against those of my own unique purposes. At times, I may legitimately regard the commands, prohibitions, or procedures of a positive law (whether of the state or of a non-state association) as having lower order value than certain claims of my own: thus if the state commands me to enter the army, I may reach the conclusion that it is far more valuable in the total scheme of things (and provided I do not forget the central command to love others as one loves oneself) for me to complete a novel or picture, even if I have to do so in jail. A human being, then, because he is a human being, will respect not only the claims of his several *social* offices or roles in possibly many groups but will also revere those of his own unique ends or goals.

Given this view, the law of the state—assuming for the

moment that we can identify it—ought not necessarily to have a higher claim on me than other rules, a point which we made earlier. In addition, however, we now maintain that the law of the state ought not necessarily to take precedence over the imperatives of my own peculiar ends, in the event of a conflict.

To be sure, we often associate state law with the effectuation of the most general good or the good common to all men; and we tend to say, therefore, that it ought to be obeyed when it conflicts with other positive laws or with what might be called the legislation I enact for myself. If, however, we remember the view of the historic state and its law advanced earlier in this treatise, then state law may or may not be compatible with some half-way approximation of the general good. In international relations, the state is notoriously a kind of special interest group fighting other special interest groups for the resources of the globe—precisely as General Motors is in competition with other corporations for the resources of the United States. Insofar as state laws reflect this special interest—as over against the claims of humanity—it is difficult to see why they should have any greater claim on me than the rules of any other special interest group. Similarly, to the degree that the positive laws of the state represent primarily the special interests of particular groups within the state, it would seem that my obligation to obey them is correspondingly lessened, other things being equal. Thus a tax law giving enormous advantages to the wealthy might be regarded as having only a very attenuated moral claim on me: perhaps if I obeyed it at all, I would do so for the sake of expediency or because I feared jail or a fine, and not because

49

I regarded that law as a matter of moral obligation.

Thus I ought to attempt to give weight in any case of conscience both to my several offices or roles in my associational life and to my role as an officer of myself. Assuming the view of personality enunciated earlier and the general obligation to respect the lives of all men "as members one of another," I am obliged in any given instance to consider all my offices or roles before making a decision. I do this through judgments about how these several roles are related to one another, to the scheme of values which seems to be most congruent with the moral order, and to the facts of a given concrete situation. When I do all these things in the widest possible frame of reference, weighing both acts of omission and those of commission, and with the most extensive testing of my tentative conclusions, I am being most conscious and acting at the highest level of conscience.

5. *Testing One's Provisional Judgments.* But how ought I to test and reformulate my tentative conclusions as to my duty under particular circumstances, and what considerations ought I to keep in mind as I go about the testing? In other words, I have a "hunch" as to what my obligation is about a given matter; but if I am to be responsible, I ought to subject it to criticism and to refine it as much as possible. This is particularly true when the matter involves obedience to law, which entails some of the most serious questions of obligation one can suggest.

In trying out a tentative conclusion, we should remember the dual nature of personality. I ought to test my tentative judgments about a problem of conscience against the judgment of others and of the groups of which I am a part—as we noted earlier in the case of the possible political assassin versus the pacifist. Although in the end I alone must make the decision, during the period of uncertainty or indeterminacy I should compare my moral experience with that of others, suggest the course of action I propose to take, and weigh the opinions of others against my own. Recognizing to what degree my moral life is beholden to others, I owe them the tribute of seriously examining their viewpoints as they bear on the conscience I am endeavoring to shape. I should have, as Jefferson put it in the Declaration of Independence, "a decent respect for the opinions of mankind."

Another way of putting this is to say that the truth should guide me. But how does one discover the truth? Here we might note a striking parallel between *scientia* and *conscientia*. We assume in science that we must compare and weigh the results of many experiments or experiences: the scientist is inseparably a part of the community of scientists which cuts across such conventional divisions as the nation and the class. Our perspective on truth may be colored by our class or our national biases, but surely our objective is to eliminate these factors which force us to see the truth only "through a glass, darkly."[26] So, too, in developing conscience, one is most apt to discover the truth of the moral order as related to particular circumstances through exchange of experiences with others.[27]

[26] I Corinthians 13:12.

[27] It is significant that Gandhi calls his autobiography *Studies in My Experiments with Truth*. Experiments would appear to mean both *experiences* which develop spontaneously during the course of life and those deliberately contrived situations that test hypotheses involving moral insights and human conduct (experiments in the usual sense of the term).

51

In the end, however, the search for moral truth in the context of a concrete case must conclude with a personal judgment, just as the quest for scientific truth cannot be decided by majority vote. After looking at a given law or custom from the perspectives of many souls, and keeping in mind my general debt to the group life of which I am a part, I must finally say "This is it"—whether the conclusion be for obedience or disobedience. Thus must Luther, following debates and public confrontations, at some stage say, "Here I stand, I can do no other." There must come a point where the indeterminacy of deliberation gives way to the determination of action—unless, indeed, one takes refuge in some unconscientious action such as mechanical following of convention, domination by fear, or unreflective submission to the pressures of the moment—whether those pressures come from groups demanding conformity or from those who call for dissent.

But just as the shaping of a scientific view entails a set of rule-of-thumb principles in working out conclusions—some scheme for testing hypotheses, for example—so the development of conscience about obedience and specific applications of obligation would appear to depend on recognition of certain considerations. In spelling these out, we are, of course, simply making explicit what is implicit in the notion of testing our tentative judgments.

Facts and Consequences. It would seem that, given an ethic of responsibility, an important requirement ought to be to obtain all the facts possible. An evaluation of any institution or rule must inevitably be affected by the scope of one's factual knowledge and one's judgment of how a given course of action is likely to shape the future. Means and ends are always interrelated, and a rejection of personal irresponsibility implies that one does not act without awareness of how particular facts, including a proposed course of action, will in all likelihood affect both oneself and others. As we have suggested, however one account for first-order or primary value premises (whether by intuition or otherwise), one's interpretation of secondary or instrumental values will be deeply influenced by the extent of one's factual knowledge.

If one is contemplating an act of civil disobedience, for example, one must somehow make a judgment not only on the character of the law itself but also on how one's potential act of disobedience will affect others and be related to one's priorities. Will it, for example, all things considered, advance respect for human life or detract from that respect? One might regard a law as stupid or, in some respects, even somewhat dubious morally, and still reach the conclusion that disobedience would create an even more stupid or immoral situation. An act of disobedience that might be fully justified on other grounds could, under given circumstances, lead to such social havoc that one might decide to reject it.

It may be objected that one never has all the facts and that projection of consequences is always very hazardous. The search for facts, the objection might continue, is usually a way of avoiding action. As for the test of consequences, it is well known that beyond a very narrow range, the exact consequences of given acts cannot be known. The immediate consequences of the Vietnamese war, it may be said, are utterly disastrous for most men—although there are degrees of that disaster, from the plight of those who are deprived of life to the burdens of those who are taxed through the ruinous and irresponsible process of inflation. The war can be defended, if at all, only by claiming that its remote consequences will tend to benefit mankind, even though its immediate effects move in a contrary direction.

While these objections have merit, they do not refute the main argument we are propounding: that one has an obligation to obtain a factual background and also an obligation to make some projection of consequences. To be sure, the facts will never all be in and the requirement could easily lead to passivity and a sense of irresponsibility. But the lack of a complete factual picture does not absolve us either from action or from gaining as good a knowledge as possible within a reasonable period of time. So too, the remote consequences cannot be known in any detail. But this does not excuse our failure to consider consequences at all.

Applying the test of consequences to the Vietnamese war, we may say that since the immediate consequences (for several years) are likely to be so horrible, we cannot envision a complex of events with immediately horrible and immoral results eventuating in a world situation running counter to the immediate consequences. Indeed, many reason in this way: Since the proximate results of a given act or series of acts are such that my moral judgments would not approve them, and since the remote consequences are beyond any exact determination, I must decide my action by putting only the immediate results into the equation. It is sometimes said that a surgical operation illustrates a contrary position: we accept immediate consequences which in nature cannot be sharply separated from cutting up meat; and sometimes, indeed, the patient is very near death. Yet we approve the operation in the hope—which, to be sure, can never be certain —that the cutting will, with the skill and knowledge of the surgeon, result in good long-run results. Here, however, our projection of long-run good results depends on our experience with previous surgery under comparable situations: we have confidence in the long-term consequences because the probability of their being favorable seems to be supported by past analogous cases. But can anyone confidently say that previous analogous cases of war of the Vietnamese type strongly indicate "good" long-run consequences for the Vietnamese conflict?

At any rate, these are some of the considerations which must be kept in mind as we insist on factual background and the test of consequences. Just when we should act, having done what we can by way of fact-gathering and projecting consequences, no formula can tell us. This uncertainty is often an accompaniment of a decision that is conscientious; and, as we shall see in our discussion of disobedience, a full recognition of the possible uncertainty accompanied by a firm determination to act may save us from the fanaticism that destroys.

Most Laws in All Probability Do Not Directly Raise Moral Issues. One can approach the question of obligation with a generalization confirmed by experience—that most laws, in all probability, do not directly raise questions which would usually be defined as of moral concern. The great bulk of the statutory and customary law in any society deals with matters turning on convenience and prudence, rather than on issues which are normally called problems of "right" and "wrong." Thus I may be irritated by antiquated legal forms which I am supposed to fill out. I may think them fine examples of the law's tendency to engage in a species of mumbo-jumbo. But the forms in themselves can hardly be said to raise questions of morality. There is no morally right side of the street on which to drive—at least so far as can be seen —and whether the law prescribes that one drive on the left or the right is and seemingly should be a matter of indifference. If I refuse to observe the law which requires that I drive on the right, to be sure, a moral question may immediately arise—for I may be putting the lives of others in jeopardy. The same would be true had legislation prescribed the left side and I chose to drive on the right. But in many spheres of life, the morally unobjectionable options for organization and rule-making are numerous.

It may be contended, of course, that even laws which are merely stupid but not morally objectionable ought to be subject both to censure and to possible disobedience. But there would appear to be an important distinction between that which is merely unintelligent and those things to which we give the designation "immoral" and "evil." Certainly the common consciousness makes this distinction and it seems to be a reasonable one. To be sure, it may be difficult to draw the line under particular circumstances; but this difficulty underlies all attempts to apply abstract distinctions to particulars.

There will be those, of course, who assert that if our vision were only wide enough, all acts and rules—however morally neutral they might seem—would take on significance. But even if this might be true from the perspective of an all-knowing God, we surely cannot see it from the viewpoint of man, which is the only approach we possess for judgments of conscience.

In determining our obligation to the law, then, we should not forget the general and supportable distinction between that which is merely stupid or causes inconvenience, on the one hand, and that which, on the other, takes on the moral quality of evil. One who is conscientious with respect to the law will not conclude that, merely because it is a nuisance for him to obey the law, he has a moral right to disobey it. Simply because the law is stupid, he is not given a license to disregard it. Even when observance of the law might cause him a certain amount of pain or anguish, he is not justified, given that fact alone, in refusing to obey.

The Prima Facie Duty to Obey Positive Law. Other things being equal, am I morally obliged to obey positive law? Ought the burden of proof, so to speak, be on those who would disobey it? Both questions should be answered in the affirmative.

Assuming that one can identify the positive law—a question about which views differ and which we shall consider presently—the law may be said to be, however roughly—and it is always roughly—a kind of social wisdom. As Edmund Burke was constantly pointing out,[28] it may be thought of as the product of the dialectic and contingencies of ages past and deserves the *prima facie* respect that one owes to factors which helped personality be born. Many medievalists spoke

[28]Throughout many of his speeches and, above all, in his *Reflections on the Revolution in France*. See, in general, Ross J. S. Hoffman and Paul Levack, eds., *Burke's Politics* (New York, 1949).

of even customary law as a type of implicit reason: it was a deposit of man's responses to challenges posed for him by general social developments. As for statutory law, it is obviously the product of deliberation of some kind, and, while subject to all the possibilities of error characteristic of humanity as a whole, is still not the result merely of "private" deliberation and untested "reason."

To be sure, we should be wary of what we are saying here. Some social scientists have seemed to suggest that because a given institution or law has survived, there must be some social or "functional" justification for it. But this is not necessarily so. Notoriously, both laws and institutions generally tend to develop a life or autonomy of their own which may be sharply divorced from the living, breathing human beings who are subject to them. Because an institution may have had a function at one stage of social evolution does not mean that it has one now; and if the original institution's goals were illegitimate—e.g., the Inquisition—its mere persistence did not give it a kind of justification.

Nevertheless, there is still a measure of validity in the argument that laws may enshrine a wisdom which superficially does not always seem to be there. And this, after all, is in major degree what we are saying when we assert that there is a *prima facie* obligation to obey the law. This is to assert that with all its inevitable shortcomings and even probable absurdities, the collective experience embodied in law is likely to embrace more facets and permutations of the human situation than my own personal limited encounters with life can include. In this sense, and to this degree only, a Burkean position has some justification.

Thus the positive law must be assumed to create an obligation to obey, unless I can show myself—after assessing the views of others and keeping in mind the considerations suggested here—that it basically and strongly runs counter to the requirements of righteousness as I have worked those out. When in doubt about whether the law does in fact run counter to moral norms, I should give the benefit of the doubt to the law.

I ought always to see it in context, too—to remember that it usually does not stand alone but is closely related to other emanations of the legal system which may cast light on its meaning and purpose. It cannot be justly regarded as a wholly isolated phenomenon, although in the end I may decide the issue of my obligation to obey in light primarily of its own particular requirements.

If I recognize a *prima facie* obligation to obey it, we must also usually assume that I acknowledge the relative legitimacy of its source and of the system which it reflects. If I conclude that I have no obligation to obey it but, indeed, a duty to disobey, this does not necessarily imply a rejection of the source or the rule-making authority; indeed *civil* disobedience implies, as we shall see, that I do accept the general system even while rejecting a particular law.

Identifying Positive Law. Throughout this discussion we have been assuming that we could identify positive law; that we could distinguish between mere custom and law, and between purported law and true law. We have, in effect, begged the question of what is law? Yet until we know what the law is (whether of the state or of non-state associations), how can we decide our *prima facie* obligation to obey? In the present section, we address ourselves briefly to this question.

How, then, can we identify positive law?

Broadly speaking, there are two positions with respect to this question. In the one, law is seen as that body of rules which is made or pronounced in a particular way, regardless of the character of those rules or of the system. In the second position, to identify law requires not only that we look at its source but that we also examine its substance; for in varying degrees, this view holds, that cannot be "law" which does not meet certain moral and logical criteria, even if it is made or pronounced in the "correct" way. The first view, then, would have us look at the origin of the statement; the second would ask us to examine not merely the origin but also the contents of the purported law and even of the system of alleged law.

In the *first position,* sometimes called the *positivist,* a statement becomes law when it is sanctioned by that person, group, or other agency in an association (and positivists deal primarily with the state) which has the authority to make or recognize law. John Austin, the great early formulator of the positivist view, identified it with the command of a political superior given to those who were regarded as political inferiors and who were accustomed to obey him (or it, if the "political superior" was an assembly or group).[29] Here law is essentially a command directed to persons who usually obey. And a keynote of positivism is that law is sharply separated from morality. Austin, as a matter of fact, insisted on this separation so that radical legal and political reform could

[29] His views are developed in his *Lectures on Jurisprudence.*

60

be facilitated: he (and his predecessor Jeremy Bentham) argued that if law were identified with that which was morally right, the psychological problem of changing it would be insuperably difficult; for how could one bring human beings to change what was somehow thought of as a dictate of the Good or of God?

But does this principle mean that if, let us say, the Mafia gets control of a nation and after three years gains general acquiescence, I am to give its decrees the status of positive law? According to Hans Kelsen, one of the great modern expositors of positivism, the answer would have to be an affirmative one: the decrees are indeed law, having proceeded from a new basic norm (*grundnorm*) laid down by the Mafia and acquiesced in, generally speaking, by the great bulk of the population.[30] The basic norm, in Kelsen's terms, is the procedure whereby subordinate legal norms (individual laws, we might say) are enacted. Thus the basic norm for the United States is apparently the Constitution; and if it should be "overthrown" by the Mafia, the latter could through its power—and if generally obeyed—establish a new basic norm that might, let us say, define positive laws as those which are decrees by the head of the Mafia alone. Looked at in another way, I can identify a statement as law if it is made by a procedure which is accepted by the bulk of the population as the method for making or recognizing law.

Legal positivism more specifically will identify positive law with any rule "created in a way provided for by the legal

[30]Hans Kelsen, *General Theory of Law and State* (Cambridge, Mass., 1945). Kelsen does not mention the Mafia, of course; but the import of his view would seem to be what we have suggested in the text.

order to which it belongs," provided that the rule "has not been annulled either in a way provided for by that legal order or by way of desuetude or by the fact that the legal order as a whole has lost its efficacy."[31] Here legal "validity" in the long run—although not in the short run—turns on "efficacy" or, seemingly, degree of acceptance by the community. Whether the legal order originated with the Mafia or Hitler or George Washington is irrelevant; rules passed according to its requirements are positive law, unless in a given instance a particular rule has been disregarded in such a widespread fashion over such a long period of time that it has lost its "efficacy."

If, then, I am a legal positivist, I determine my *prima facie* obligation to obey law by identifying law with all those rules —regardless of their particular character—that have been passed according to procedures laid down by a system of norms which itself is widely accepted. In other words, if the *source* of the alleged laws is accepted by the great bulk of the community, the emanations of that source are also law—at least if they are usually obeyed. If I accept a positivist view, I identify law by asking myself what most men think of as law; I would then regard myself as having a *prima facie* obligation to obey it.

Although positivists usually identify law with state law, there is no reason why their general principles cannot be applied to the identification of law in any association. Thus if I am to determine the law of the Roman Catholic Church, being a member of that body, I will ask what the great bulk of Roman Catholics regard as the basic norm of Roman

[31] *Ibid.*, p. 120.

Catholicism and then ask whether an alleged law has been passed according to that basic norm and has been generally obeyed by Roman Catholics (efficacy) over a period of time. If it meets these tests, it is *prima facie* entitled to obedience by me, if I am a member of the Roman Catholic Church.

So, too, the source of law in the Amalgamated Union of Carpenters is that which is generally regarded by the Carpenters as the source, whose particular laws are generally obeyed. If I am a member of the Carpenters, *prima facie* obedience will be due to all such rules. If there is a formal change in the way laws are made, I shall, of course, have to accept the laws emanating from the new source as *prima facie* claiming my obedience. If there is a "revolutionary" change too—let us say a gang from the Cosa Nostra seizes control, alters the rule-making authority, and is generally recognized by the Carpenters over a period of time—as a positivist, I will now recognize as the basic norm that which the revolutionists have proclaimed.

Shifting back to state law, the positivist view is nicely illustrated if we turn to the rise and fall of the Nazi regime. In gaining power, the Nazis originally observed all the formal requirements of the Weimar Republic, although strong-arm tactics early began to be used in order to get votes.[32] After he was installed as Chancellor in 1933, Hitler dissolved the Reichstag, and the subsequent elections witnessed intimidation, which resulted in solid ostensible support of the regime

[32]Hitler was careful to observe the *forms* of the law while violating its spirit. Later on, of course, when he was in firm control, he pushed through a captive Reichstag a radically different procedure for making law—one in which he himself could decree law.

63

in the Reichstag. Thereupon, Hitler began to change the way laws were to be proclaimed, and the laws which were issued under the new basic norm took on characteristics (discrimination on grounds of race, for example, and wide latitude given to the judges to interpret the laws according to "blood and soil" emotions) widely different from the positive laws of the previous regime. Yet if I had been a Jewish legal positivist living in the Germany of 1936, I would still have had to regard these rules as law and therefore as *prima facie* entitled to obedience. Regardless of their *moral* character (given my insights into the moral order) and even if they demanded the shooting of all Jews without trial, there could be no question in my mind as to whether they were law or not; and the burden of proof morally would be on me to show that my *prima facie* obligation to obey should be overturned.

So far as one can see, in other words, the legal positivist would recognize as a law-making authority any man or group of men—regardless of the methods they used or their own personal characters—whose decrees were generally obeyed (whatever the motive—fear, sense of obligation, self-interest, and so on).

According to the *second* or *non-positivist* view, alleged systems and purported particular laws have to meet certain moral standards before they can be entitled to the designation "legal systems" or "laws." Actually, the non-positivist position has many sub-schools and there is a wide diversity of interpretation as to the moral standards that must be observed. What might be called traditional natural law would tend to say that the system must have a modicum of "rationality" before it could be regarded as the source of particular laws; and a given purported law, to be law, must be, in the words of St. Thomas Aquinas, "an ordinance of reason, for the common good, made by him who has the care of the community, and promulgated."[33] Here the requirements are that the rule be "reasonable"—which would seem to mean that it must have a rational purpose, make classifications that are not arbitrary, and use means which comport with reason; that the over-all objective be the "common good"—rather than particular interests; that the rule be proclaimed by a legitimate ruler (not a tyrant); and that it be made public— a rule not made public would presumably have no binding legal effect, even though it met the other three conditions.

In modern times, a narrower view of "natural law" has been suggested by men like Professor Lon Fuller.[34] Generally speaking, he argues that the very idea or definition of "law" entails that the statement possess certain characteristics (such as, for example, that it not command opposite things and that its categories and classifications not be arbitrary) which, if they are not met—either in the legal system as a whole or in particular laws which are the fruit of the legal system— destroy its quality as law.

If one is not a legal positivist, then, it would seem that identification of positive law will depend on one's judgment as to the *moral* legitimacy of the system itself (which the positivist will insist is an irrelevant question) and on the degree to which procedures prescribed by the system are

[33]St. Thomas Aquinas, *Summa Theologica,* IA-II-ae, Question 90, 4.

[34]See, for example, Lon L. Fuller, "Positivism and Fidelity to Law," 71 *Harvard Law Review* (1958), pp. 471-505.

observed in adopting a particular rule. It will also depend on the conformity of the rule to certain moral norms, even if the rule has been passed in accordance with the procedures laid down by the system. Thus, generally speaking, one might give moral approval to the system but find a particular rule emanating from the system morally obnoxious: hence, such a rule would not be "law" even though adopted under the acceptable system.

Stated in another way, the issue between the positivist and the non-positivist is one of what statement shall have the honorific title "law." Since this term traditionally has been held in respect, and even in awe, both positivists and non-positivists think that it is extremely important to identify it. The fact that a particular statement is regarded as "law" is in itself persuasive for many persons; and, indeed, we have argued here that there is a *prima facie* obligation to obey it.

We may illustrate the difference between positivists and non-positivists by citing an incident from the Nazi era. The case involved a series of National Socialist purported laws providing for punishment of those who might criticize prominent leaders of the National Socialist Party. In 1944, during a leave from the German army, a soldier criticized Adolf Hitler to his wife and said that it was too bad the Chancellor had not been killed in the plot of that year. The wife reported his words to the police, who arrested the husband and took him before a court which sentenced him to death. The death sentence was not carried out, however, and after spending a short time in jail, the soldier was sent to the front. When the Nazi regime collapsed, his wife was arrested and charged with bringing about the illegal imprisonment of her husband. Her defense was that she had acted under the statutes passed by the German government and was simply performing her legal duty. The court overruled the plea of the defense and declared the statute not a law, thus permitting the punishment of the wife for securing the false imprisonment of her husband.

Was the Nazi statute a law? If it was, then presumably the wife had a legal defense. If it was not law, by what process of reasoning could the judge reach his conclusion?

Legal scholar H. L. A. Hart, a positivist, condemns the German court for refusing to accept the defense plea. The court had ruled that the alleged statute was "contrary to the sound conscience and sense of justice of all decent human beings." Although admitting that the act of the wife was morally repugnant, Hart contends that the Nazi law was, after all, "law" in the positivist sense of the term. If the postwar Germans had wished to condemn her, they should have passed a retroactive law making her offense a crime after the act had been committed; for although retroactive laws, Hart admits, are always evil, they are a lesser evil than the confusion of law with morals. The German courts, by failing to distinguish between law and morality, contributed to the clarification of neither.[35]

By contrast, Lon Fuller, with his natural-law-like bent, thinks that on the whole the German court acted rightly. Although not accepting fully the extreme "higher law" doctrines apparently admitted by the postwar German judiciary, he maintains that there is an "inner morality" of law itself

[35]H. L. A. Hart, "Positivism and the Separation of Law and Morals," 17 *Harvard Law Review* (1958), pp. 460-62.

which, if seriously violated by the system or by particular alleged legislation, destroys the legal character of a statement. Thus German courts under National Socialism very often disregarded their own proclaimed statutes and appealed instead to "reason of state." If this kind of activity becomes ubiquitous —as it did, Fuller argues, in Hitler's time—the very notion of a legal system is denied and with it any obligation to regard particular alleged laws as laws in fact. For law cannot arise outside a legal system; and if the administrators of an alleged legal system habitually treat it with contempt, particular emanations of the system cannot be regarded as law.[36]

An educated conscience under Hitler would, no doubt, have engaged in an inner dialogue having elements of both Hart and Fuller as well as of other thinkers who have attempted to provide criteria for identifying positive law. The Hart-like side could have termed Hitler's decree a "law." The anti-Hart position might have reasoned in a number of different ways. It might conceivably have denied the moral legitimacy of the system, according to some natural law approaches, thus making the effusions of the system "no laws." Or, with Fuller himself, it could have maintained that countless alleged statutes were so widely disregarded by the courts and administrators as to deny the very minimal definition of a legal scheme, thus making a particular statement non-legal and hence creating no *prima facie* obligation to obey. Alternatively, an alleged particular statute might have been seen as violating basic moral principles, although the non-positivist might still see the Hitlerian system as a legitimate source of law in general.

The implication of the Hart-like view would have been that

[36]*Op. cit.*, pp. 480-81.

the rule, while positive law and hence entitled *prima facie* to obedience, was morally bad law, thus raising the question of any moral obligation to obey. The import of the non-positivist position might have taken several forms. If the legal system itself was regarded as non-existent because morally outrageous or because it did not really constitute a *legal* system (according to Fuller's definition), then any emanation of the alleged system was equally tainted—and the statement would not be entitled, given our principles, to *prima facie* obedience. If the supposed authority was somehow accepted as legitimate and the statement was adopted in accordance with the principles of the authority, the purported particular law would be regarded as law and hence entitled *prima facie* to obedience.

Those who regarded it as law would assume, unless they could convince themselves of its serious moral flaws according to the principles we have suggested, that it should be obeyed. The burden of proof would be on them to show that it should *not* be obeyed. Those of the non-positivists who did not think of it as law at all would not have to consider it, *prima facie,* as binding. The existential results of the two positions, however, might be the same; for while the positivists might think of it as law, they might also see it as morally outrageous and hence not to be obeyed; while the non-positivists might consider it as no law at all and thus to be disregarded. Both the positivists and the non-positivists would probably end up in jail or lose their lives.

Whether one denominates a rule "bad law" or "no law" makes relatively little practical difference, except that those who assume the former stand have the burden of proof to show to themselves that it *is* bad law. The positivist who concludes that the statement is bad law, and, after careful consideration, decides to disobey it, is in essentially the same position as the non-positivist who contends that the alleged law is "no law." While the latter will not be disobeying a "law" according to his own lights, he will still be disregarding what most persons consider law. Both the positivist and the non-positivist will be disobeying that which the great mass of humanity probably think of as a law, although the attitude of the non-positivist will be that he is technically not disobeying a "law," since he himself does not think of the statement as having that honorific designation.

Positivist and non-positivist alike, however, are posing for us the broad question of disobedience in general and, implicitly, the issue of revolution. To these problems we now turn, keeping in mind our discussion of conscience, our treatment of ambivalent attitudes to law, and our analysis of obligation.

IV. OF DISOBEDIENCE AND REVOLUTION

The legend of the Fall of Man can perhaps illustrate the many-sided consequences which have resulted from obedience and disobedience since that far-off time when Eve is supposed to have tempted Adam, who succumbed to her—and therefore disobeyed—without very much resistance.

The original refusal to obey was, of course, a violation of the direct command of the Lord, which, while perhaps not positive law, was somewhat analogous to law. Paradoxically, the disobedience not only opened up the floodgates of evil but also made it possible for man to develop the arts, create civilization, and, indeed, to become a mature human being with individuality and the dilemmas arising in connection with multifarious choices. Man had to rebel in order to become a person and to disobey that he might develop autonomy; but in the very act of rebellion and disobedience and in the very process of becoming a person, he planted the seeds of disaster as well as creativity.

Our First Parents' disobedience undoubtedly made possible all the details of evil. Thus it led to death, to melancholy, and to our consciousness of finiteness. We could no longer revel in the innocent state with a belief in natural immortality. Then, too, the disobedience revealed a loss of humility and a development of the full implications of pride. With pride went lust—concupiscence of the eye, concupiscence of the

71

flesh, and pride of life, as the medievalists used to say; and lust tended to be accompanied by a corruption of rationality, by the quest for power over other human beings, and by war. Finally, at least according to one version of the Fall, man's first disobedience gave birth to civil institutions, with their restrictions, their bureaucracy, their tendencies to oligarchy, their frequent violations of human personality.[37] Had man obeyed in Eden, he would have been saved from these disastrous fruits of the Fall. But since our First Parents insisted on disobeying, they had to accept the onerous penalties ordained by a loving and a just God.

On the other hand, continued obedience would have left them in the state of little children. Their autonomy would have been still-born and their experiences would have remained one-dimensional instead of many-dimensional. Disobedience, while it opened the floodgates of evil, was also a prerequisite for creativity and for the civility appropriate to human beings. Although the Fall led to death, the very awareness of finiteness was necessary for man to judge and reflect on life; and some men have taught that it is consciousness that our bodies will perish which helps reinforce the civility without which we could not become persons. A child knows death, and therefore life, only superficially; mature men, as they become conscious of disintegrating bodies, can gain a below-the-surface appreciation and understanding of life. So, too, with the lust which arose after the Fall. While on the one side it tends to obscure

[37]This was certainly the central medieval interpretation of the Fall, down to the thirteenth century at least. Stemming from St. Augustine, it pervaded the writings of the early canonists and was used as a propaganda device by papal apologists in their struggles with temporal rulers.

rationality and to open up the probability of war, imperialism, and slavery, on the other side its very presence stimulates the conflict, both intellectual and social, without which achievement cannot take place. The existence of lust means that no claimed authority—civil, ecclesiastical, or military—can ever be measurably pure; and while tainted authority may be essential in man's historical state, it is always tending to become the spokesman not for the general weal but for special interests and for power as an end in itself. General Motors is perennially trying to identify its interests with those of the public good; and deputy secretaries of Defense are frequently amazed when critics deny that ownership of $300,000,000 of stock in a defense industry can be compatible with impartiality in an official position.

Becoming aware of the fragility of kings, presidents, popes, and prime ministers suggests the necessity, on occasion, for disobedience and resistance, if rulers' lusts are to be checked. All claimed authority over other men is—as we have seen St. Augustine suggesting—afflicted from the very beginning with the corruption of the robber band. On the other hand, it is equally true that those who repeat the disobedience of Eden, this time in order (at least in part) to check an all too fallible human rule, have within themselves real potentialities for making their very disobedience the occasion for their own striving after dominion. Thus Lenin revolted against tyranny and became a tyrant himself. If in some sense, however, the Fall gave birth to the external restrictions of civil institutions, it also opened up the way for knowledge of the good, the true, and the beautiful in their many dimensions: after all, the fruit which Eve and Adam consumed in the Garden came from the tree of the knowledge of *both* good and evil.

But because of this very fact, every achievement of good is accompanied by the possibility of equivalent evil. Thus the original disobedience prepared the road for complex technology but at the same time made it possible for men to become slaves to what they had created. It laid the foundations of cities but with those foundations went a comparable danger —that urban civilization would stifle man and lead to his physical and psychic disintegration. Disobedience multiplied choices, but its lusts threatened men with destruction of all choices. It made for greater practical freedom and for the law or non-arbitrary rule which accompanied that freedom; but it also provided the basis for a tyranny which was utterly unknown before the disobedience. It unlocked the door for what we call the "conquest" of sub-human Nature, but it also created the conditions for a wounded Nature to react violently when pressed beyond endurance. It established the framework of an enormous enlargement of human consciousness, but it also tempted man to believe that he could play God with impunity. It made men aware of the need for personal humility only to tempt them to succumb to the probability of corporate and national arrogance.

Now when disobedience is shifted into the context of civil and historical society, it is confronted with problems which arise out of the original disobedience. No historical civil society or claimed authority has ever escaped the results of the Fall and, hence, cannot be said to have been worthy of obedience under all circumstances; on the other hand, no act of disobedience, however justified, could ever be without its own perils: arrogance, lust for dominion, ethical nihilism, and

74

similar fruits. While civil authority and law are goods, they are never so authoritative as to exclude a vindication of disobedience under given contingencies. After all, if disobedience against the Lord opened up possibilities for knowledge of good, surely disobedience of the less-than-divine rulers of history could presumably have equal or greater benefits. Obedience, too, may have merits, as in Eden. Both disobedience and obedience may be duties. But under what circumstances and within what limits? To questions of this kind we now turn.

Assuming that one has followed our previously stated considerations in reaching a conscience about obedience to a claimed law in a particular instance, and assuming further that one's conclusion is for disobedience (if one is a non-positivist, one's disobedience may be to a statement which many others, if not oneself, may regard as law), what principles should one observe in implementing this disobedience?

The classic answer, of course, was that of Socrates, whose position might be phrased as one of following one's conscience, even though that might entail prosecution, but at the same time not attempting to evade the penalties of the law.[38] It would seem that Socrates is telling us that we must on occasion violate a given law (as the rule is interpreted by existing administrators and judges) but that we must also recognize the *principle* of lawfulness by accepting the sanctions attached to violation of the law. The same or essentially the same position was taken by John Locke (at least in matters involving religion), assuming that the ruler is acting within the

[38]In Plato's *Crito*.

75

limits of his general authority.[39] A reading of Martin Luther King's letter from Birmingham Jail[40] indicates that he espoused a similar view; and it is well known that King's exemplar, Mohandas Gandhi, had endorsed it on many occasions. More recently, former Justice Fortas has eloquently restated the argument.[41]

It has about it the aura of reason, since it would seem to acknowledge both the notion of respect for law in general and the idea that, given the nature of law and human society, on the one hand, and of human personality and conscience, on the other, there will be times in which the individual can do no other than commit acts of civil disobedience.[42] It recognizes both the social and the trans-social dimensions of the soul and seeks to make the best of the clashes that will inevitably occur between conscientious men and what may be unusually unjust laws. It makes a clear and useful distinction

[39]See his *Letter Concerning Toleration*.

[40]Martin Luther King, "Letter from Birmingham Jail," in *Why We Can't Wait* (New York, 1964).

[41]Abe Fortas, *Concerning Dissent and Civil Disobedience* (New York, 1968).

[42]The recent literature of civil disobedience is considerable, including, for example, Hugo Bedau, "On Civil Disobedience," *Journal of Philosophy,* LVIII (1961); Charles Cohen, "Essence and Ethics of Civil Disobedience," *Nation* (March 18, 1964); Charles Frankel, "Is It Ever Right to Break the Law?" *New York Times Magazine* (January 12, 1964); Mark R. MacGuigan, "Civil Disobedience and Natural Law," 52 *Kentucky Law Journal,* 364 (1964); Mulford Q. Sibley, "Direct Action and Integration," *Hastings Law Journal* (February, 1965); Mulford Q. Sibley, "On Political Obligation and Civil Disobedience," *Journal of the Minnesota Academy of Science* (v. 33, No. 1, 1965); and Rudolph H. Weingartner, "Justifying Civil Disobedience," *Columbia University Forum* (Spring, 1966).

between evasion and conscientious civil disobedience.

Its implications are that once a person decides he must disobey, he will do so publicly, non-violently, and with intent to benefit the community or mankind, rather than merely himself. In accepting the penalty attached to disobedience, he is paying homage to the *principle* of positive law and lawfulness in general, while protesting and resisting a particular law.

The American Civil Liberties Union has defined civil disobedience as "the willful, non-violent and public violation of valid laws because the violator deems them to be unjust or because their violation will focus public attention on other injustices in society to which such laws may or may not be related."[43]

George Woodcock has analyzed in a helpful way the significance of the word *civil* in civil disobedience. He suggests that it means, among other things, that the justification for civil disobedience is to be found partly in the idea that the citizen who commits it is fulfilling his responsibilities to society; he is not, in other words, rejecting his civil obligations. Secondly, Woodcock goes on, the word is to be contrasted with "military," which evokes the image of physical force. The civilly disobedient reject the appeal to physical force. Finally, "civil" is related to "civilized behavior." A certain courtesy is owed even to enemies and most assuredly to our fellow-citizens who may not agree with us.[44]

But a problem arises if we take the usual definitions of civil

[43]*Civil Liberties*, monthly publication of the American Civil Liberties Union (December, 1968), p. 1, column 3. See the article "Disobedience Vote Taken."

[44]George Woodcock, *Civil Disobedience* (Toronto, 1966), pp. 3-4.

disobedience literally. They imply that the disobedience is to a law—though a bad one—which has been recognized as such by the person who is disobeying. Implicitly, they seem to accept a positivist view of law. Suppose that the individual is a non-positivist and views a particular alleged law as "no law" because of its moral character (and not because he claims it is "unconstitutional"). Is he committing an act of civil disobedience when he disregards it? After all, in his view, he is violating no law. In the technical sense, perhaps, he is not engaging in civil disobedience. But here we are assimilating his act to that of the civilly disobedient and shall regard him as committing civil disobedience if his act is in pursuit of conscience. When, for conscientious considerations, he violates that which most men regard as law and observes all the requirements for civil disobedience, we shall view him for our purposes as also committing civil disobedience.

Another issue arises in nations which, like the United States, have a procedure whereby the courts can declare an alleged law in violation of the basic law or constitution. In such instances, the legal test can be made only by a person violating a claimed law in the hope that the courts will agree with him that the law is "no law." Technically, such an act would not be one of civil disobedience, since the claim before the courts is that the purported statute is not in conformity with a more basic positive law. Although the violator has much in common with the civilly disobedient, and often acts in his spirit, he is making essentially a *legal* and not a *moral* claim (although the two may happen to coincide). But while such a person is not technically a civilly disobedient person, as we have been using the term, we should keep him in mind because of his close proximity to the position outlined here.

Generally speaking, the civilly disobedient continue to accept the view that aspirations for justice are present in the legal system as a whole, even when particular segments of the system may seriously violate or distort those aspirations. Socrates did not reject the basic norms of Athens, and, because he did not, he thought he had an obligation to accept the punishment attached to a particular rule which he could not conscientiously observe. Those who committed disobedience in the Civil Rights struggle of the United States were not advocating a complete uprooting of the existing general principles of law and society; rather they were violating particular laws because they either (a) supposedly ran counter to the Constitution itself; or (b) so offended the resisters' sense of morality that they could not be observed. To be sure, the line of distinction between, on the one hand, disobeying a particular law either because it is unjust or because disobedience will symbolize a larger injustice and, on the other, rejecting the very premises of the legal system, is often a thin one. But provisionally, at least, it would seem essential to maintain the distinction, which appears to be vital as a basis for distinguishing *civil* from various forms of *uncivil* disobedience.

The Varieties of Civil Disobedience. Going beyond the formal definition a bit, we may observe that in the past civil disobedience has been at times individual in nature (as with, for example, Henry David Thoreau) and on other occasions has been concerted or mass. When individual draft resisters refuse to register or to report for induction, without much of a common plan, the act is individual and, according to some definitions of the term, "non-political." The individual seeks to preserve his own integrity or to protest injustice but does not necessarily intend to effect an immediate change in policy. When individuals act in concert to violate a law, it may be regarded as mass civil disobedience and frequently has an avowed political objective. Thus, when Gandhi led his famous march to the sea during the thirties, it was to violate the salt monopoly laws; and the whole disobedience was planned far ahead of time and highly organized.[45]

Mass civil disobedience can also be termed "conspiratorial" in one sense, even though "conspiracy" is often associated in our language with secrecy. The late H. G. Wells used to speak of a potential and desirable "open conspiracy" against war makers throughout the world;[46] and while his conception embraced more than the idea of mass civil disobedience, it certainly included that notion.

We may also distinguish between direct and indirect civil disobedience. In the former, the law itself is regarded as unjust or is closely connected with a particular injustice. In the latter, the law may not be regarded as unjust, but the disobedient may feel they have to violate it in order to protest some injustice effectively and dramatically—as when it was proposed that traffic to the New York World's Fair be impeded (thus violating the traffic laws) in order to dramatize and

[45]See Krishnalal Shridharani, *War Without Violence* (New York, 1939). See also Joan Bondurant, *Conquest of Violence* (Princeton, 1958).

[46]H. G. Wells, *The Open Conspiracy* (New York, 1928).

protest the injustice of racial discrimination and segregation.[47]

Civil Disobedience, Protest, Non-Violent Resistance, and Revolution. A mark of man's complicated estate since the Original Disobedience is the fact that there may be many forms of dissent and protest and that, usually in the heat of discussion, we frequently confuse them with one another. On the one hand, there are forms of dissent and protest which may be perfectly legal—strikes, many kinds of boycotts, demonstrations, petitions, violations of long-standing customs (as contrasted with law), public denunciations, and many forms of non-cooperation. Technically, too, as we have seen, a deliberate violation of claimed law under the belief that the law is unconstitutional is not an act of civil disobedience.

On the other side of the spectrum we have "revolution," whether violent or non-violent. Here civility itself may be breached at one or more points on grounds that the political and legal system as a whole must be repudiated: one's obligations to be "civil" supposedly cease when the very foundations of the system—as contrasted with the justice or injustice of particular laws—are attacked. Thus many have argued that when the very idea of civility is repudiated by claimed guardians of an alleged law, the dialogue implied in technical civil disobedience cannot take place and the only resort is revolutionary activity, violent or non-violent. Obviously, revolution would constitute a gigantic act of disobedience, but it would hardly be "civil"—at least in the full meaning of that term—in the sense suggested here.

[47]And there were many other similar cases, some of which involved technical violations of trespassing ordinances.

Thus civil disobedience stands somewhere between legal forms of dissent and resistance, on the one hand, and revolution, on the other. Mass civil disobedience, other things being equal, is usually closer to the pole of revolution than its individual form. From one point of view, civil disobedience is relatively conservative, whatever those may say who denounce it. What forms dissent *should* take will obviously depend on many factors, including the circumstances of particular situations. Now, however, we turn specifically to the justification for civil disobedience, as over against vindication of legal dissent and revolution.

Of the Justification for Civil Disobedience. There are many who would make the grounds or occasions for justifying civil disobedience very narrow indeed. Thus we find former Justice Fortas ruling out the permissibility of *any* indirect civil disobedience, when he says:

In my judgment, civil disobedience . . . is never justified in our nation, where the law being violated is not itself the focus or target of the protest. So long as our governments obey the mandate of the Constitution and assure facilities and protection for the powerful expression of individual and mass dissent, the disobedience of laws which are not themselves the target of protest—the violation of law merely as a technique of demonstration—constitutes an act of rebellion, not merely of dissent.[48]

Others would go even further and deny the moral legitimacy of *any* civil disobedience, direct or indirect, in a supposedly democratic society like that of the United States. Thus Senator

[48]Abe Fortas, *op. cit.,* p. 124.

82

Mark Hatfield appears to maintain that, while deliberate violations of law may be defended in other societies, they are never supportable here.[49] Former Solicitor General Erwin N. Griswold has taken a similar stand. The American community, former Dean Griswold argues, "maintains sufficient legitimacy so as to be entitled to insist that its lawful commands be obeyed."[50] If the constitutional rights of the minority to dissent have been respected, he goes on, the minority "must accept the voice of the majority and abide by the [valid] rules."[51] Disobedience of laws which, on their face, are legally valid, Griswold contends, cannot be supported, since dissidents have had adequate access to the normal channels of communication.

While many, including former Justice Fortas, seem to think that civil disobedience in a "totalitarian" society may be justified, they are often rather vague as to the precise standards we should adopt in deciding when we should disobey. Critics of civil disobedience, on the whole, are reluctant to contemplate it (at least in their own societies) and often seem unwilling to recognize the ambivalent position or status of law which men like Plato and St. Augustine frankly faced.

On the other hand, the tone of some comment—that of Harris Wofford, for example[52]—seems to take delight in the

[49]Mark Hatfield, *Not Quite So Simple* (New York, 1968), Chap. VII, "Civil Disobedience," pp. 98-106.

[50]Speech delivered before the Biennial Conference of the American Civil Liberties Union, June 24, 1968, *Civil Liberties,* No. 256 (July, 1968), p. 1.

[51]*Ibid.*

[52]See Harris Wofford, *Which Is the Danger:Civil Disobedience or Undue Obedience?* (mimeographed)—talk to the session on "Protest in a Democratic Society," 91st Annual Meeting of the American Bar Association, Philadelphia, August 6, 1968.

thought of disobedience. If ancient Athens, asks Wofford, "was a great steed that needed a gadfly to sting its conscience, don't our colleges and universities and churches and corporations and cities and nation states need such a gadfly?"[53] We are told, in language reminiscent of John Stuart Mill, that the danger is really not too much disobedience but rather too little. Both dissent without civil disobedience and dissent through civil disobedience ought to be cherished; and it is not infrequently implied that, like the original disobedience in Eden, civil disobedience at times may be a prerequisite for creativity and enlarged knowledge.

We have already suggested our general position, having contended that there are times when—given the general nature of claimed law and authority—the individual conscience, acting deliberately and reflectively, must consider the obligation of disobedience. We have contended, moreover, that the individual must ultimately be the judge of those laws he must obey or disobey, even though there is a *prima facie* obligation to obey, assuming that the law can be identified.

Those who argue that civil disobedience is always illegimate in so-called open societies are wrong. They err in frequently implying that "open society" models—those, presumably, in which one can work for change of laws through peaceful methods and in which one's power to effect change is substantially equal to that of others—actually exist in the historical scene. Even if such societies did exist to a greater degree than today, their laws conceivably could command acts that might overturn *prima facie* obligations to obey: an individual might still regard a law as so unjust that to obey it even

[53]*Ibid.*, p. 5.

84

temporarily would be seen as an undermining of his basic integrity. For example, he might believe, with most of the early Christians, that service in the army was one of the greatest sins he could commit. It would be a mockery to tell him that he must first commit this heinous sin and then—after his conscript term had expired—work for a change in the law.

Actually, of course, there are no truly open societies such as are postulated by Justice Fortas. In form, to be sure, they may not be closed; but when one considers the distribution of power, change in the law through normal methods is often impeded for very long periods. To be sure, one may grant that there is a significant difference between a society like that of Britain, on the one hand, and of Nazi Germany, on the other. But when that is admitted, we must still contend that even where the processes of "orderly" change are open in a nominal sense, they are so frequently time-consuming and severely limited by the social and economic structure that correction of evils solely through "establishment" channels is sometimes well-nigh improbable. In the United States, for example, where the distribution of economic power has not changed basically and substantially since World War I (the upper 10% of income recipients get about 30% of the income —27% to 28% after taxes— and the lower 10% only about 1%; in 1910 it was 2%), to say that those in the lower 20% of the population are equal in power for social change to the upper 20% is to say what is manifestly untrue.

All this affects profoundly the way in which political power is utilized and makes it enormously more difficult than would otherwise be true for the lower third of the population to have any substantial effect on policy. The tax laws, by and large,

85

as written and administered, favor the rich and the well-born; the Selective Service System is in effect shaped to work against the poor and powerless; access to important public office is (whatever the formal theory) open only to a few professional men who can afford the risks and then only if they can acquire large amounts of money; black and Indian persons are still systematically excluded from large areas of economic, social, and political life; publication of newspapers is heavily weighted in favor of those who share orthodox viewpoints and possess education, organization, and wealth; radio and TV stations are largely the prerogative of self-interested corporations; the renting of public halls is often carefully restricted to exclude expression of unorthodox opinions; redress through the courts, while ostensibly open to all, is actually, and in considerable measure, available largely to those of education and financial means; and even where the machinery of redress is supposedly available, it frequently consumes so much time that those seeking justice give up in despair. Everywhere, the oligarchical tendencies of organization under complex division of labor work against ostensibly democratic and liberal forms.

In all this, of course, one simply sees reflected results of our First Parents' disobedience. In the very process of creating "civilization" with its presumed benefits, we tend to enslave ourselves to our own creations; and in seeking with all good will and intelligence to reduce the element of fortune and chance in human affairs—through the planning and deliberation we call politics—we are always tending to inflict inequities of a new kind. We simplify law and endeavor to eliminate its anomalies only to find similar excrescences growing up under new guises.[54] We begin with a measure of social equality but in the process of developing economies and civilizations establish new and sometimes more onerous inequalities.

Because of tendencies like these, Thomas Jefferson argued that even ostensibly liberal and semi-open societies needed not merely civil disobedience but actual "revolution" once every generation. If Jefferson can defend revolution, it would seem that every generation can surely envision civil disobedience as an option, and oftentimes as a significant duty. If, as Nicholas Berdyaev argued,[55] all complex organization enslaves, then at certain points individuals must assert their claim to freedom by limiting the enslavement through rebellion— an important theme of Albert Camus' great novel *The Rebel*.

The critics are right, to be sure, in suggesting that no act of civil disobedience, however carefully weighed, is without difficulties. Every act, as a matter of fact, is a venture not only in rationality but in faith. The assessment of one's intentions, as well as the judgment of consequences, cannot be implemented without pain and suffering. But this is true of conscientious obedience as well of conscientious disobedience. We often emphasize the difficulties of the latter and ignore those of the former, since so much of our obedience is slavish and the result of a kind of compulsive conformity: we do not think critically about obedience and hence do not even become aware of its problems.

[54]This seems to be the history of codification. For a time it appears to simplify and make comprehensible what has hitherto been confusing. But then interpretations of the code and uncertainties as to language increasingly introduce new confusions.

[55]See Nicolai Berdyaev, *Slavery and Freedom* (New York, 1944), and *The Realm of Spirit and the Realm of Caesar* (New York, 1952).

In thinking critically about disobedience, it is important to recognize a distinction which has been suggested but not yet emphasized: the difference between acting primarily to preserve individual or personal integrity, on the one hand, and on the other, becoming disobedient in order to change the structure and practices of society. Both may on occasion be fully vindicated, given the framework we have suggested.

Many of the early Christians are good examples of civil disobedience committed primarily to preserve personal integrity. So far as we know, they were not concerned about social reform, since most of them believed that the end of history was near.[56] While most of them recognized an obligation to obey what they recognized as the law of the state—with both Peter[57] and Paul[58] earnestly teaching conformity for conscience' sake—at the same time they also believed that "one must obey God rather than man"[59] in the event of a conflict between divine commands and merely human decrees. When, therefore, they were commanded to sacrifice to the genius of the Emperor—a rite which in their view was religious, although the Romans apparently regarded it as purely civic—they simply refused, with no expectation that they could

[56]See C. J. Cadoux, *The Early Church and the World* (Edinburgh, 1925), and Amos N. Wilder, *Eschatology and Ethics in the Teaching of Jesus* (New York, 1939).

[57]I Peter 2:17: "Honor all men. Love the brotherhood. Fear God. Honor the King."

[58]Romans 13:1-2: "Let every soul be subject unto the higher powers. For there is no power but of God: the powers that be are ordained of God. Whosoever therefore resisteth the power, resisteth the ordinance of God: and they that resist shall receive to themselves damnation."

[59]Acts 5:29.

change the world by doing so but with a firm intention of recognizing God's decrees as supreme. This attitude was reflected, too, in the rejection of military service by such young men as Maximilianus (A.D. 295).[60] Maximilianus clearly exhibits many typical early Christian views: he speaks of "this age"; and he foresees its imminent end. He evidences no hope of changing the social structure through his act. Nevertheless, he cannot serve in the army, since to do so would violate God's commands not to kill or to sacrifice to idols. Maximilianus' attitude is clearly reflected in the writings of the great early Church Fathers, who state the inherent incompatibility of military service with Christian teaching.[61] When Maximilianus was killed by the state for his refusal to kill, he felt he was preserving the integrity— or wholeness, or health—of his soul, even though he lost his body; but he had no direct political objective.

In our day, sects like Jehovah's Witnesses have committed civil disobedience for considerations very similar to those of the early Christians. Like Maximilianus, they believe in the imminent end of history, conceive of their actions as pursuant to commands of Jehovah, and are not concerned with transforming the social order.

The context of much civil disobedience in our time, however, is often social and political. While the problem of pre-

[60]The transcript of Maximilianus' trial is reprinted in Adolph von Harnack, *Militia Christi: Die Christliche Religion und der Soldatenstand* (Tübingen, 1905), pp. 114-117.

[61]Among the Fathers who held service in the army to be incompatible with Christian faith were Origen, Tertullian, Clement of Alexandria, and Lactantius. For a lengthy discussion of their attitudes, see Cadoux, *op. cit.*

serving personal integrity is never far away, it is also hoped that the deliberate violation of law will shake up the social structure in desirable ways. The statement of a modern draft resister at the time of his sentencing to a four-year term will illustrate this point. He resists, he says, in order to make his actions conform to his beliefs, whereas, on the whole, most moderns actually serve the "almighty dollar" rather than the God to whom they pay lip service. But he resists also in order to provoke change in the social order: "To achieve a sense of morality and concern, and then to transform that sense into an effective political force, some laws, including the Selective Service Laws, must be openly and non-violently disobeyed at every possible opportunity."[62]

And another resister strikes about the same note. He sees himself as part of a larger social movement which will expand dissent in general:

> I believe it's necessary to escalate dissent from mere criticism to peaceful, non-violent civil disobedience; refusing to serve in the military when called with the willingness to face the alternative of going to prison.[63]

It is also true, of course, that very few acts of civil disobedience in our day are undertaken without serious misgivings and doubts. Thus Gandhi always thought of disobedience as a last resort—as the final stage in non-violent direct action. It came after petitions, boycotts, legislative activity, self-purification, and agitation. He was always particularly concerned about mass civil disobedience, lest violence break out

[62] Statement of George Crocker before the Federal District Court, St. Paul, Minnesota (mimeographed), March 18, 1969.

[63] *Minneapolis Tribune* (September 4, 1968), p. 1.

on the periphery of the movement.[64] At the same time, he thought that disobedience properly carried out could be one of the most moral and efficacious of political methods.

Martin Luther King was likewise troubled, for he clearly saw the apparent contradiction involved when Negroes demanded, on the one hand, that the desegregation laws be implemented, and, on the other, deliberately violated certain laws themselves. Thus he spent a whole night weighing the issue of a specific disobedience and sought to defend his action in his eloquent *Letter from Birmingham Jail*.[65] To be sure, he concluded, he would be violating an injunction of a court in holding his demonstration; but he pointed out—among other defenses—that Southern society was in essence a closed community[66] and that the judicial injunction has been a favorite device in Southern states to forbid what would in other circumstances be perfectly legal forms of protest.[67] Like Gandhi, King was worried by the common charge that civil disobedience, whatever the intent of those who used it, always encouraged violence.[68] Hence he insisted on rigid discipline and in Birmingham is said to have remarked: "I want 5,000 supporters, not 10,000, because I don't believe that there are that many non-violent Negroes in this city."[69]

[64]See Shridharani, *op. cit.,* and Bondurant, *op. cit.*

[65]Martin Luther King, *op. cit.*

[66]For an analysis of this thesis with respect to Mississippi, see James W. Silver, *Mississippi: The Closed Society* (New York, 1964).

[67]King, *op. cit.,* p. 70.

[68]Thus Mark Hatfield, *op. cit.,* pp. 101, 103, argues that "The riots of the summer of 1967 are in some part the harvest of civil disobedience . . ."

[69]Quoted by Simeon Booker, *Black Man's America* (Englewood Cliffs, N. J., 1964), p. 53.

The two causes which were the occasions for most American civil disobedience during the sixties, support of Civil Rights and opposition to the Vietnamese war, were certainly defensible from the viewpoint of the doctrine of obligation stated earlier in this treatise. Those who committed disobedience in their name could, and did, put forward a powerful vindication.

We have already touched at several points on the Civil Rights struggle. Here we need only recapitulate the considerations which supported those who took drastic action. Much of the United States was not an open society, and the creed of equality professed so widely was violated in wholesale fashion. Deliberately excluded from the franchise in many parts of the country, blacks had little political recourse in the orthodox sense of the term. Often their legal rights were denied by administrators themselves; and even when the law was very explicit in protecting them, judges and executives were lax in their implementation of the rule. To those who asked them to wait, the civilly disobedient quite rightly replied that they had waited more than three hundred years. The shock of civil disobedience was at least one way to show the white power elite that there were forms of non-violent power which even the poor and the helpless possessed. Civil disobedience was designed to bring practice into accord with professed ideals; and, together with other forms of direct non-violent action, it greatly advanced this objective.

As for justification of civil disobedience in connection with the Vietnamese war, it is only necessary to recall certain salient facts about the war and its context to make a powerful case for deliberate violation of the conscription and other laws involved. For one thing, the war was never declared by Congress, contrary to the specific requirements of the Constitution; yet it was difficult to get the courts even to consider this issue. A prominent international lawyer argued, moreover, that the war clearly violated the United Nations Charter.[70] The conflict was escalated contrary to all campaign pledges of the President: In October, 1964, he was saying that American boys should not fight it; but no sooner was he safely inaugurated than he began to demand that they do so. These breaches of law, democratic procedure, and political morality—aside from pacifist or other bases one might cite—are weighty enough in themselves to raise the question of whether one has not merely a right but also a duty to disobey. There should be a certain reciprocity or fair play between a government and citizens; and if this is seriously breached by one side—and particularly by the government, which has such enormous power vis-à-vis the citizen—surely this may be said to reduce the obligation of the other. One can plausibly quote Immanuel Kant at this point: "No one is bound to refrain from encroaching upon the possession of another if the latter does not in equal measure guarantee that the same kind of restraint will be exercised with regard to him."[71] And this, to reiterate, would be only one consideration that could help justify civil

[70]Arthur Larson, "Power and Law in World Affairs," *The Progressive* (November, 1966), p. 14. Larson cites particularly Article 37 of the U.N. Charter. Another noted student of international law, Quincy Wright, also argues that the war is clearly in violation of the Charter. Note Marcus G. Raskin and Bernard Fall, eds., *The Viet-Nam Reader* (New York, 1965), pp. 7-12.

[71]Immanuel Kant, *The Metaphysical Elements of Justice,* trans. by John Ladd (Indianapolis, 1965), p. 71. See also John Rawls, "Legal Obligation and the Duty of Fair Play," in Sidney Hook, ed., *Law and Philosophy* (New York, 1964).

disobedience. The peculiarly outrageous moral character of the war itself could be added—the employment of anti-personnel bombs designed primarily to injure people rather than buildings; the use of gases; the destruction of crops needed to support life; the callous burning of villages, and so on.

Because powerful reasons have existed to support civil disobedience in connection with Civil Rights and the Vietnamese war does not mean, of course, that every particular act of disobedience is necessarily justified. While the general moral right and even duty might be maintained, a given act, depending on context and circumstances, may be of dubious legitimacy. Thus college students isolating Navy or Marine recruiters in their car and forbidding their egress, although an act of civil disobedience, might with some justice be regarded in this particular context as questionable.

Often it seems to be assumed in discussions of civil disobedience that because passive acquiescence may involve little apparent disturbance, it is therefore somehow more nonviolent. Most conformity to law, unfortunately, is in the nature of passive submission rather than of active conscientious obedience. But is passive acquiescence always to be exalted over disobedience—with its controversy and divisiveness? Actually, it would seem that apathetic obedience may in the long run be a greater source of violence than either active obedience or civil disobedience. Passive acquiescence assumes rather indifferent citizens, who are unconcerned with the social evils which tend inevitably to develop in large, complicated, and bureaucratic societies. The longer these evils fester, the more likely they are to provoke eventual violence in reaction. A society which aspires to freedom and "democracy," as

John Stuart Mill argued,[72] needs citizens who actively and conscientiously obey rather than those who acquiesce passively or with reluctance. Passive acquiescence or slavish obedience cannot advance either the cause of non-violence or that of democracy. Possible civil disobedience is the price we must pay if we are to develop the ideal of active rather than tamely passive citizenship.

We can illustrate our point by recalling the examples of societies in the past. Suppose there had been widespread civil disobedience by students under the German Weimar regime —disobedience directed against the use of Article 48 of the Constitution (emergency powers) and economic disintegration.[73] Would not the rise of Hitler have been less likely? Suppose that during the early years of the Hitler regime, millions of Germans had civilly disobeyed certain laws in protest against anti-semitism. Is it not possible that the power of Hitler would have collapsed? To be sure, many of the civilly disobedient might have been imprisoned or shot; but it is inconceivable that widespread and disciplined disobedience would not have proven a very powerful political weapon. Or imagine that, instead of waiting until the winter of 1917, millions of Russians had disobeyed in, let us say, 1915. Is it not probable that a substantial change without violence and the dictatorship of the *Bolsheviki* could have taken place?

These questions are asked to point up the enormous significance of conscientious disobedience for life in general. While

[72]In *Representative Government.*

[73]Increasingly, in the years immediately before Hitler's appointment as Chancellor (1933), German governments had resorted to Article 48 of the Weimar Constitution, which meant that they could rule by decree on the plea that there was an "emergency."

we should always be aware that disobedience has its own perils—as we have suggested earlier—the dangers of passive and unthoughtful obedience are at least as great.

The perils of passive acquiescence include a decline of awareness, the growth of apathy, confirmation of slavishness, and loss of sensitivity. Attenuation of conscientiousness is both the root and the fruit of passive acquiescence. In Eden, the distinction between passive acquiescence and conscientious obedience did not exist, for problems of conscience (aside from the one Great Temptation) had not yet arisen. With the Fall, however, the temptation passively to obey other men came to be as great as the temptation to disobey compulsively or for primarily egoist ends—indeed, the former temptation was probably greater. Both passive obedience and compulsive disobedience reflect our First Parents' original sin. Passive acquiescence may be said to represent an implicit desire to reject freedom and responsibility; while unconscientious disobedience may denote a concentration on one's own ego and a rejection of the social bond.

The great bulk of mankind has been unable to emancipate itself from either passive acquiescence or ego-centered rebellion. Conscientious and discriminating obedience, on the one hand, and civil disobedience, on the other, are mirrors of our attempt to sustain sensitivity and awareness of the many elements which enter into the life of man as he seeks to grapple with his fallen state: his involvement with others, as well as his transcendence of the group; the necessity for law, yet its ever-present inadequacies; the value of order, but the perils inherent in the specious kind of order built on passivity; the fact that potentialities for creativity seem always to be accompanied by equally real possibilities for destruction.

Nor would the duty of civil disobedience cease with the formation of a World State. The same conflicts of loyalties, the same ambivalence with respect to law, the same problems of conscience about obligation and obedience would exist. Indeed, all these phenomena might conceivably be even more acute. The pretentiousness of organization appears to increase with size and complexity; and the dangers of idolizing organization in the form of a World State, and hence of being enslaved by it, might be magnified. Whatever the merits of a World State in relation to the preservation of peace—and those merits have been greatly exaggerated, especially when we recall that some of the bloodiest conflicts have occurred *within* nation states—it is probable that it would tend to demand of us that unqualified obedience which consciences rightfully could not give. Its thrust to oligarchy and bureaucracy would no doubt resemble that of the nation state (although the absence of external "enemies" might restrict this tendency in some measure) and this thrust could be checked, in the end, only by readiness not merely for legal dissent but also for civil disobedience.

But whatever the context or occasion for civil disobedience, we should reiterate that it ought not to be adopted without the searching inquiry which we outlined earlier. Civil disobedience attempts to affirm rationality and civility in a world which often discounts them; and for it to take place without careful weighing of obligation would be, in a sense, a contradiction of its objectives—if, indeed, we could even call it civil disobedience under those circumstances.

Having made our decision to disobey, we should be willing

—within the context of civility—to accept the penalty, even if not eager to do so. We disobey in the name of justice; but we accept the penalty to help preserve the principle of lawfulness. We disobey because we have concluded that disobedience will enhance righteousness; but a part of the righteousness we endeavor to preserve is respect for law. Although it has been maintained by some that the civilly disobedient do not have this respect, it can plausibly be argued that they demonstrate greater veneration for law than those who obey mechanically and without thought; for the latter, in grounding their conformity on uncriticized habit, appear to take the purposes and means of law with less seriousness than the conscientiously disobedient. It is somewhat like automatically agreeing with everything a certain person may say: we show far less respect for his mind and soul under such circumstances than if we listen carefully, weigh his words, and, when conscientiously impelled to do so, express vigorous dissent. And it is certainly obvious that those who conscientiously disobey show greater respect for law than those who disobey for egoistic ends, or for revenge, or without deliberation.

Harris Wofford rightly points out that much of our evaluation depends on our attitude to law. If we see it simply as arbitrary command or a kind of fixed factor, rather than as a rather provisional and tentative statement purporting to govern conduct, our relationship to it will be one of mechanical obedience without understanding. But the law, Wofford goes on, should be seen not merely as a command but also as a question:

> Inherent in every law there is the possibility that some citizen will judge it to be unconscionable. . . . In this view,

every law . . . is always asking every citizen affected by it the question whether it is a just and good law. And if the citizen's answer is No, then there is always the alternative of civil disobedience.[74]

The disobedient, he correctly observes, are carrying on a kind of dialogue with those administering the law—and out of the dialogue may conceivably emerge a greater understanding of the demands of righteousness on the part both of the disobedient and of the judge. This in itself contributes to those aspects of civilization that can be regarded as creative.

If we see civil disobedience, moreover, as in part a kind of recapitulation of our First Parents' defiance, we may view it as a recognition of the perils inherent in both obedience and disobedience. Uncritical obedience stultifies the individual and contributes to tyranny in the state—whatever the form of the latter may be. On the other hand, a general spirit of uncritical disobedience undermines the basis of group solidarity and, in the end, given the close relation of person to group, can become a factor in personality disintegration.

Man after the Fall has an unfair advantage over his First Parents: he sees that while his own creativity is due to the Original Rebellion, the conditions necessary for social life and therefore for human life impose strict limitations on the kinds and quality of disobedience. Our First Parents could not have foreseen this. Disobedience after the Fall may be essential to check many of the tendencies due to it—aggrandizement, for example, and bureaucracy, tyranny, materialism—yet in the very act of disobeying, the disobedient, without recognition of limits, may be creating similar dangers in different

[74]*Op. cit.,* p. 5.

form. The civilly disobedient who are sophisticated are under no illusion that theirs is the Final Disobedience, after which there will no longer be any necessity for it. Rather do they envision their disobedience as part of an ongoing and never-ending dialectic of deeds, in which the enslaving tendencies of organization and the injustices of particular laws are opposed by conscientious refusals to submit; while, at the same time, the potentialities for new enslavements in the future are recognized.

The Question of Direct and Indirect Disobedience. Earlier, in defining types of civil disobedience, we made a distinction between direct and indirect disobedience. Here we raise the problem of justification. Is it legitimate to violate laws which have little or no relation to the injustice that one is protesting? It may be quite right, the objector to indirect civil disobedience may urge, to refuse to obey a law prohibiting "miscegnation," but how can one justify obstructing traffic to a World's Fair as a way of protesting the racist society? Or, to take other examples, can one defend illegal occupation of a legislative chamber in order to protest absence of action by the city council on fair housing; or young men and women chaining themselves to the pillars of public buildings in New York to attack lack of federal measures on race in Mississippi;[75] or hundreds deliberately occupying and blocking entrances to a large city hotel to compel the hotel manage-

[75]*New York Times* (October 15, 1964), p. 35. The incident occurred on the portico of the United States Court House at Foley Square. Each chained demonstrator had a large letter affixed to his mid-section, and together the letters of the demonstrators spelled "Freedom Now."

ment to eliminate alleged discrimination in hiring practices?[76] In each of these instances, the laws violated (traffic rules, statutes against trespass) apparently had almost no direct connection with the moral offenses alleged.

But in justifying disobedience it would seem to be difficult to discover a hard and fast distinction between its "direct" and "indirect" varieties. As usual, much would depend on the particular circumstances. Using the fundamental criteria we have suggested earlier, including respect for human life in all of its manifestations, there are certainly occasions in which indirect disobedience would appear to be supportable. The fact that it *is* indirect, however, does suggest that it has an additional handicap and that there is a greater burden of proof on those who would commit it than on those who violate a law which they believe to be grossly unjust in itself.

The Problem of Individual and Mass Civil Disobedience. Some would appear to make the distinction between individual and mass civil disobedience a crucial one. The contention would seem to be that the former may arise out of a justifiable conscientious conviction but that the latter is merely "political." It is difficult, however, to sustain this argument. Surely an act of collective civil disobedience—for example, the violation of the salt laws in India[77] and many of the American Civil Rights movement's defiances of law—can be as conscientious and as justifiable substantively as any act of individual protest. It may be contended, of course, that the consequences of the collective act may be radically different

[76]*New York Times* (March 19, 1964), p. 23.
[77]Shridharani, *op. cit.,* and Bondurant, *op. cit.*

from those entailed by purely individual resistance. This is indeed true: mass civil disobedience, persisted in on many occasions, has implications that many would call "revolutionary" (as did Gandhi's mass civil disobedience campaigns). But then we have argued throughout that in weighing obligations to obey the law under any circumstances, a responsible decision always requires consideration of the consequences as one of the factors. Those, moreover, who set "political" or mass civil disobedience over against individual breaches would often seem to be accepting without serious criticism the notion that moral can be sharply separated from political concerns.

It is true, of course, that large-scale civil disobedience runs the risk that many may participate simply because of social pressure or merely because of a charismatic leader. There is always the danger, too, that "mob psychology" will take over. These are factors which must be seriously weighed. But their possibility should not in itself exclude a possible adoption of mass disobedience if on other grounds it can be sustained.

The Obligations of Officials. The act of civil disobedience occurs within the limits of civility and rationality and seeks to preserve the principle of lawfulness while violating particular laws. If the civilly disobedient recognize the obligations inherent in this context, officials and judges confronted with the problem of civil disobedience have certain obligations, too. While judges, no doubt, must impose penalties, yet it would seem that if they can, within the limits of the law, take into account motivation and intention and conscientiousness, they should adjust the penalties accordingly. That some judges do in fact recognize a distinction between conscientious and non-conscientious disobedience of law is well known. Thus one federal judge virtually apologized to a draft resister in sentencing him to two years in the penitentiary. His fellow judges were sentencing men convicted of similar offenses to four years. This judge however—rightly, according to our argument—thought of conscientiousness as a mitigating circumstance.[78]

Nor is this a novel principle. For years, many nations have made a distinction between "ordinary" and "political" criminals, the former being classified as those who violated the law merely for economic gain or revenge or for other selfish ends, while the latter breached legal rules conscientiously and for what they hoped would be the common good. If one robs to feed one's family, it is still a violation of law; but surely the principle of civility would require that the purpose of the robbery be considered a mitigating circumstance, not only for the sake of the violator but also for the good of a society which in some sense aspires to economic equity and is aware of its deficiencies and self-righteousness.

Administrators and judges, moreover, act against a background in which they themselves sometimes select the laws which they will implement. In certain instances, administrators simply ignore statutes which are on the books, even though they are sworn to apply them. Their considerations in doing so are various but are frequently non-conscientious. When the chief justice of a large state and leading member of its board of pardons was asked recently why the board did not record in writing its reasons for denying pardons—which is

[78]The remarks of Judge Earl Larson are quoted in the *Minneapolis Tribune* (September 4, 1968), p. 1.

specifically required by law—he admitted that the law was violated again and again by the board, but defended the violation on the ground that to state reasons in writing would be inconvenient.[79] The chief justice admitted his law violation; but countless administrators are hardly as open. This is not to say that occasional law violations by administrators in themselves justify acts of civil disobedience. All we are asserting is that, in view of the non-conscientious breaches committed by the guardians of the law, it would seem particularly incumbent for judges to place conscientious violations of law in a different category from non-conscientious ones.

In general, we are not arguing for any particular system of penalties—indeed, some might argue that deliberate, conscientious violations ought to incur stiffer penalties precisely because the act was premeditated and conscientious—but rather for the principle of distinguishing between conscientious and non-conscientious offenses. Earlier we suggested that there was an important difference between a pattern of conscientiousness and one not characterized by conscience. Here we are simply suggesting that this distinction be recognized officially by communities which themselves aspire to civility. This means, among other things, that while the substance of the conscience's deliverances is always of great importance for the moralist, the law itself and its administrators should recognize conscience as such, whatever its substance.

[79]Chief Justice Oscar Knutson of the Minnesota Supreme Court, when asked why the Board of Pardons did not, as required by law, give written reasons for denial of a pardon—and the Chief Justice was the "dominating figure" on the Board of Pardons—explained: "We just don't have the time to write them all down. It may be the law, but it's not our practice." *Minneapolis Tribune* (March 8, 1969), p. 8.

This might take several forms: specific provisions for conscientious objectors to given laws might be one; the law's allowing the administrator to take account of conscience might be another. To the degree that laws attempt to do this, a community is exalting the principles of civility.

Law-makers, administrators, and the civilly disobedient, if they act in this way, will be conscious both of the corruption always present in law and administration and at the same time of the relative justification for law. They will also understand the mixed character of disobedience—on the one hand, as frequently essential to preserve personal integrity and to check injustice; with law and its administrators, on the other hand, as containing within itself those very potentials for the injustice which its practitioners are protesting. When civility is exalted, within the context of the human condition as we have described it, the possibilities for intellectual and moral progress are great; and acts of official administration and disobedience alike can be instruments of that progress.

Hard Cases and the Problem of Revolution. The notion of *civil* disobedience is, of course, a model or standard. Any given act of conscience that results in disobedience may fall short in some measure of the norm of civility. To recur to an early example: Smith, let us say, reasoning from the principle of the Golden Rule and holding to the principle of the sacredness of human life, concludes, nevertheless, that under given circumstances he can do more to preserve life in general if he assassinates a public official who is widely regarded as a tyrant. If he proceeds to carry out the assassination—and assuming he has followed principles of deliberation we have outlined—he is certainly violating law for conscience' sake, but his act of disobedience is hardly non-violent. He surrenders to the authorities and confesses, avowing as his motive the public good (and the context of his life indicates that he has probably stated his motive correctly). He has committed an act of disobedience which is in many respects civil but is certainly not an exemplification of pure civil disobedience.

Or consider a conscientious abolitionist living in the North before the Civil War. He is asked by a fugitive slave to assist him in fleeing to Canada. If the abolitionist agrees, after wrestling with his conscience, his act of defiance must necessarily be secret: he could hardly invite the authorities to observe him. After the slave has reached Canada, the disobedient person can, to be sure, surrender to the authorities, take the penalty, and avow his legal offense. For the most part he has been civil, as we have used the term. Yet the act itself was carried out in secret: while it was not evasion for private gain, it was certainly not open defiance. The act of disobedience had to be carried out in such a way as not to imperil the slave. To be sure, the abolitionist might have been some kind of a non-positivist in terms of legal theory and might have argued that the Fugitive Slave Law was "no law." But certainly it was regarded as law by most Americans and basically the problem of civil disobedience was raised.

Cases such as we have cited here can perhaps be called ones of quasi-civil disobedience. They are expressions of conscience carried out in such a way that respect for lawfulness is essentially preserved, even while particular laws are violated. The case of the assassin illustrates that what we suggested earlier is often true: that one might begin one's reasoning

106

with some commonly held general principle—e.g., respect for life or the Golden Rule—and still develop a conscience quite at odds with that of most men. When the deliverances of that conscience also violate one of the principles of civility —even though most of those principles are observed—there comes to be a conflict between what one's conscience demands and what, in part, civility requires. The second case illustrates a similar principle: in the very act of carrying out one's conscience, civility is breached at one point—this time with respect to secrecy.

There would seem to be no escaping hard cases of this kind. Confronted by them, what are the duties of judges and administrators? If we follow our argument suggested earlier, they cannot be classified as ordinary "crime"—although they are certainly criminal acts. They are to be differentiated from non-conscientious breaches of the law by reason of the fact that, while those who committed the acts were not completely civil in their disobedience, the limitations on their civility were inherent in the consciences they were attempting to follow. This fact ought certainly to be taken into account by judges confronted by their acts.

Always there will be hard cases of this kind, for historical experience can never be categorized in the concrete without many ragged edges. About all that one can say is that, generally speaking, the principles of civil disobedience ought to be observed if we value lawfulness and yet at the same time recognize that one ought to follow one's conscience. Civil disobedience is the form of resistance which is most nearly compatible with upholding both the value of lawfulness and order in general and the rights of individual conscience.

Beyond a certain point, of course, the whole problem of revolution and its justification is raised. When the political system is challenged at its foundations, we may say that a revolutionary situation exists. The system's "legitimacy" is so discounted that the dialogue supposedly characteristic of civil disobedience appears to be inappropriate. An example often cited would be Nazi Germany. Here rulers systematically and extensively disregarded the rules they themselves had made— this occurs to some degree in every system, of course—and the alleged laws made little effort to strive after the non-arbitrary but instead enshrined at their center the irrational and arbitrary. Under such circumstances, a respectable intellectual tradition would hold, the very definition or idea of "lawfulness" has been corrupted and what purports to be an expression of civility has become its opposite. To be sure, positivists held that the system was still a "legal system"— but even they often argue that it was a bad legal system. As for non-positivists, Lon Fuller[80] has stated that a scheme like that of the Nazis does not possess the minimal elements of lawfulness to justify its being called a "system" of law. Every purported legal system, to be sure, has elements of the piratical in it, as we have contended. But there comes a point where differences in degree become distinctions in kind, and where

[80]There is no sharp separation between the "is" and the "ought," Fuller argues. Law, to be law at all, is always striving to achieve certain purposes, and the purposes cannot be arbitrary or unreasonable. A "system" of law must have a minimal coherence and consistency to be a system at all; and when consistency, coherence, and similar qualities break down beyond a certain point, the alleged laws flowing from the system break down with it. See Lon Fuller, *The Law in Quest of Itself* (Chicago, 1940) and *Problems of Jurisprudence* (New York, 1949).

the system itself—and not merely particular expressions of it—seems either, with the positivists, to be a thoroughly bad legal scheme, or, with the non-positivists, no legal system at all. Such, for many at least, was the framework of National Socialism.

Rudolph H. Weingartner has offered other considerations for regarding National Socialist society as "non-civil" and therefore as inappropriate for "civil disobedience" in the strict sense of the term. He points out that attempted civil disobedience, under conditions such as those prevailing in National Socialist Germany, would in all likelihood have provoked great violence; since consequences must always be considered in developing a conscience on the subject, anyone proposing civil disobedience ought to have borne this in mind. Moreover, "if the punishment for breaking the law can be expected to be extremely severe, the commission of civil disobedience (always assuming other things to be equal) is less justified, for we have duties to ourselves as well as to others. And from the consideration of these consequences for bystanders and actors follows a corollary that seems paradoxical." And he concludes:

Still, it is true that where the agents of the state—the police and the judiciary—are cruel and punitive in the extreme, civil disobedience is not likely to be justified. In Nazi Germany of 1940, say, civil disobedience would have been pathetically inappropriate: a certain minimum level of civilization must be attained before civil disobedience can be justified; below it only evasion or rebellion—or acquiesence—are justifiable.[81]

[81] Rudolph Weingartner, *op. cit.*, p. 43.

Whether or not Weingartner is right—and many might question his argument—he illustrates the proposition that there is a line to be drawn between *civil* and *uncivil* disobedience; and that while, in general, the former ought to be preferred as long as there is even an element of hope in the system, there may come a point where revolution or uncivil disobedience or what Weingartner calls rebellion should be considered. Earlier we said that civil disobedience is really a moderate or conservative position to take in relation to conscience and the law. It attempts to reconcile our qualified obligation to obey law with our very important obligation to act conscientiously. But if the whole system and its potentialities are questioned at basic levels by the conscience, one seems implicitly to become a revolutionary.

Had Socrates reached the conclusion that the very basis of Athenian life had become so corrupted that he could no longer identify himself with it, he presumably would have been justified in escaping—an act of conscientious evasion, we might say, rather than of civility. If the very principle of lawfulness is viewed with contempt by the system itself, the disobedient do not show respect for law by accepting the penalties. They appear, in fact, to be sanctioning lawlessness and the rule of sheer arbitrary force. Under such conditions, it would seem— and again we might refer to Kant's principle of reciprocity[82] —one would appear to be released from any obligation that might be associated with the notion and value of lawfulness. It might not only be permissible but an obligation to evade and escape.

To be sure, uncertainties and difficulties abound in devel-

[82]*Op. cit.*

oping a conscience about the subject. Let us recall, for example, the situation of Gandhi in India. He insisted throughout that disobedience must be *civil,* even though his objective was the elimination of British rule—which, from some points of view, and under some definitions, might be considered a revolutionary objective. Through a combination of certain circumstances and the use of many diverse methods, including civil disobedience, the British were eventually induced to turn authority over to the Indians; and the transition was carried out according to legal forms. The change was a fundamental one, by many definitions—and hence "revolutionary"—yet the methods in the struggle implied a sufficient respect for the existing colonial system to make *civil* rather than *uncivil* disobedience obligatory.

What becomes of the principle of non-violence when uncivil undermining of a tyrannical system appears to be justified? Here judgments will obviously differ. Some will argue that when civility is breached at any point, there is no sound justification for retaining any of its elements, including the idea of non-violence. The various theories justifying tyrannicide argue that any moral imperative against taking human life —particularly the life of the tyrant—is suspended.[83] Or, in other terms, all the principles of civility are abrogated: the revolutionary disobedient or rebellious are justified in utilizing any means; for, after all, tyranny by definition recognizes no moral limits. Not only may the disobedient surreptitiously violate the alleged law and evade the penalty but they may also deliberately take the lives of the tyrant and his minions.

[83]See the discussion in Oscar Jaszi and John Lewis, *Against the Tyrant* (Glencoe, Ill., 1957).

But while this is the view still predominately held, there is good ground for doubting it, and we argue here that it should be rejected. Throughout we have contended that the notion of obligation to others begins with the general principle of respect for human life. This respect is disregarded at our peril, even in a revolutionary situation. To be sure, we have recognized that a person may begin with the general principle of respect for human life and still conscientiously conclude that in given circumstances he must kill a few precisely in order to implement the respect for life. But although we may agree that this view can be dictated by carefully developed conscience, we think it is a wrong conscience. The principle of non-killing, while certainly embraced within the notions of civility and lawfulness, goes beyond them. The command not to take human life deliberately would appear to be about as close to an absolute as one can discover in the existential world. And it is a command to respect life not only under "normal" conditions but also in the supposedly exceptional circumstances (such as tyranny) which to some appear to justify a breach of the general principle. In doing harm even to one's enemy, as Socrates argues in the *Republic,* one is destroying his manhood and at the same time deteriorating one's own respect for the idea of humanity and righteousness.[84]

[84]*Republic,* Book I. The concluding statement of Socrates in his dialogue with Polemarchus reads: "Then if a man says that justice consists in the repayment of debts, and that good is the debt which a just man owes to his friends, and evil the debt which he owes to his enemies—to say this is not wise; for it is not true, if, as has been clearly shown, the injuring of another can be in no case just." Although this statement is not entirely clear, it would seem to exclude deliberate killing, even of one's enemies. It is difficult, of course, to reconcile with the continued existence of war in the *Republic.*

What is more, the resort to killing and to what is sometimes called deadly force, or violence, is of doubtful value as a means if the end be freedom or the achievement of righteousness. One cannot, to be sure, prove without doubt that resort to violence inevitably hinders moral progress—there are too many variables. But the history of modern so-called revolutions—the French, for example, and the Russian—seems to lend credence to this view. Even when violent revolution eliminates a particular tyrant, it tends to establish newer and often more onerous forms of tyranny; for the resort to violence puts a premium on leaders who are skilled in its manipulation, and once men submit to them they tend to become the victims of their own destructive means. At the very least, we can say that while violent revolutions may incidentally attain some good, the price they exact is enormous and probably disproportionately great.[85] It is like burning down houses to produce roast pig, as in Lamb's classic essay.

We may place the problem of "revolutionary violence" within the framework of our First Parents' disobedience. Given that disobedience, with its resulting limitations on human means, it is impossible to use deliberate killing and violence for good ends. While God may make even wickedness to praise him, man cannot do so. Yet man is constantly tempted to think of himself as God and thus to repeat the Fall. Only when he ceases to pursue the frustrating methods of violence, and begins to recognize fully that neither civil nor uncivil disobedience can promote good unless their practi-

[85]On the social and other costs of violent revolutions, see D. W. Brogan, *The Price of Revolution* (New York, 1966).

tioners recognize certain basic limits, can man make significant progress against tyranny.

All this does not mean that mankind is utterly helpless against lawless and tyrannical regimes. On the contrary, man's rejection of violence—even when confronted by foreign or domestic tyranny—eliminates the temptations which violence brings with it and frees him to pursue more efficacious means. He can then seek to alienate the servants of the tyrant from their master and undercut his power at its roots. Man can offer the collective disobedience which, without violence, has constituted so potent a weapon in the past.[86] While methods of this kind also have their price, both the moral and the physical cost would seem to be far less than that attached to violence; and the probabilities of restoring a reasonably legitimate and lawful regime would be much greater. Violence and the notion of lawfulness are so basically opposed to each other that when disobedience becomes uncivil it should at least cling to non-violence.

[86]Non-violent resistance may take many forms, legal and illegal. The pressures of street demonstrations and economic boycotts may fall into the former category. Collective refusal of taxes, some boycotts, and widespread rejection of service in a conscript army are examples of the latter. Escaping from the country, which may be legal or illegal, may be said to constitute another form of resistance. In "revolutionary" situations, of course, one might presumably be evasive in carrying out resistance, although, if the argument of the text has validity, one would not kill persons. For an analysis and examples of non-violent types of resistance in general, see, for example, Mulford Q. Sibley, *The Quiet Battle* (Boston, 1969).

V. CONSCIENCE, LAW, DISOBEDIENCE, AND THE FUTURE

Let us now briefly recapitulate what we have said and ask about its relevance for the future of conscience, obligation, and law.

We have argued that the distinction between conscientious and non-conscientious conduct is significant, regardless of whether we approve the substance of the conscience. We must judge an act, then, in terms of its conscientiousness as well as of its specific contents: both are at the bar of judgment. The notion of conscientiousness embodies rationality, concern for others, a striving after consistency in conduct, and a recognition both of "absolute ends" and of consequences as criteria for righteousness. Conscientious conduct is to be contrasted with thoughtless, erratic, selfish, and careless behavior. Men may agree on general principles for conduct while disagreeing about specific applications; while rationality and comparison of fundamental experiences of value can carry them to agreement in most instances, there will be times in which two equally conscientious men may feel they have to take diametrically opposed positions with respect to a concrete problem of conduct.

As it confronts law, a conscience ought to weigh the role of law in human affairs and see it in perspective. If it does so, it will neither idolize law nor show contempt for it. On the one hand, law by its very nature can never do perfect justice, both because it is an instrument that has to classify men—treating these unique creatures as if they could be placed into a few broad categories—and because it reflects orderings which always have something of the piratical about them. On the other hand, law is much better than tyranny, which, given the nature of man, is its usual alternative.

Informed by this perspective on law, what, then, must a conscientious person do before deciding whether or not to obey it? He must recognize that he alone can answer this question for himself; he alone, if he is to be free and responsible, must decide which laws to obey and which to disobey. But in making this decision, he should recognize that he is intimately connected with other human beings, that personality could not develop except in the group (while still transcending the group), and that every individual owes to the human group a debt for his very being. Obligation is rooted in the primary value notion that we should be grateful for the gift of human life. But obligation is many-fold: to oneself, to others, to the groups of which one is a part, to the state. Because the conscientious man values human life and human life is inseparable from the group, and because law is an expression of this group solidarity and the need for common expectations, he will, on the whole, respect the principle of lawfulness—though recognizing the ambivalent position which law holds. In fact, assuming that he can identify positive law, he will have a *prima facie* obligation to obey: that is, the burden of proof is on him to show that he should not obey.

But in deciding whether or not he should obey, his conscience must be informed: he must be clear about his own

116

value system—whether it be based on natural law, on a Kantian ethic, or on some version of the Golden Rule or other scheme; attempt to use reason as far as it will carry him; try to utilize the criterion of consequences, while admitting the difficulty of assessing them; and test his provisional conclusions against the experiences of his friends before making his decision. If he decides that he must disobey, he should attempt to be civil—that is, to act publicly, to be willing to accept the penalty and to be non-violent. Administrators have a corresponding obligation to civility when implementing the law. In a sense, administrators and the civilly disobedient are carrying on a kind of dialogue about righteousness and law; and out of this dialogue could emerge progress in understanding, given good-will.

But civil disobedience is many-faceted. Relative to revolution, it is conservative. It may be obligatory to engage in it simply to preserve one's personal integrity. Or it may also be used as a device for social reform, to shock the power structure. It may be individual or mass; direct or indirect. Obviously, there are many dilemmas confronting those who would be civilly disobedient: the problem of engendering violence, even though the act itself is non-violent; the issue of discipline, if it is a matter of mass disobedience; the question of when precisely civil disobedience does and ought to give way to revolution. From one point of view, civil disobedience reflects many of the roots and fruits implicit in our First Parents' defiance. It has its own perils—the danger, for example, that it may fade into compulsive or nihilistic disobedience. The laws which the civilly disobedient challenge may reflect gross injustices; but the implications of disobedience, too, may, without a sense of limits, lead to equally great injustice. Both the administrator and the civilly disobedient inherit the problems of Eve's defiance. Both passive acquiescence and compulsive disobedience are to be spurned, yet the temptation is always present to succumb to them.

When the minimum conditions for civility have disappeared, in terms of one's judgment of the legal-political system rather than of particular laws, then the justifiability of "revolution" is posed. The framework of civility—even the minimum present in historical societies after the Fall—may be gone. But if one opts for revolution, as something more than civil disobedience, it would seem that at a minimum the principle of respect for human life must be preserved. Indeed, effective resistance to tyranny can best take place non-violently.

As mankind confronts the future, there seems to be little possibility that the problems of obligation, obedience, and disobedience will disappear. Indeed, the obligation of disobedience may become even greater if and when a World State arises and the possibility of escaping to another civil society does not exist. The establishment of the World State will not in itself guarantee either peace or justice. Many of the same issues that confront us in nationalistic and war-making societies will continue to challenge us. The tendency to oligarchy and tyranny in organization will need periodic shocks if it is to be checked; and growing conscientiousness, with willingness to commit acts of civil disobedience or even to engage in non-violent revolution, holds out the possibility of keeping laws closer to the norms of justice and the state less piratical. If conscientiousness, in the sense we have been defining it here, should grow, the problems of administrators with respect to dissenters might grow with it; for if larger numbers obey conscientiously rather than passively, it is also probable that greater numbers would also disobey conscientiously. And with both acts and the administrative responses to them will go the possibilities of creativity and progress, on the one hand, and of destruction and moral degeneration, on the other.

But how, given the nature of the human soul and its involvements in past and contemporary social life, could it be otherwise?